Natural Environment Research Council

Institute of Terrestrial Ecology

Spartina anglica – a research review

ITE research publication no. 2

Edited by
A J Gray and P E M Benham

London: HMSO

COVER ILLUSTRATIONS

Extensive area of *Spartina anglica* following invasion, with (inset) a clump in its vigorous, invasive phase
(Photograph A J Gray)

The INSTITUTE OF TERRESTRIAL ECOLOGY (ITE) is one of 15 component and grant-aided research organisations within the NATURAL ENVIRONMENT RESEARCH COUNCIL. The Institute is part of the Terrestrial and Freshwater Sciences Directorate, and was established in 1973 by the merger of the research stations of the Nature Conservancy with the Institute of Tree Biology. It has been at the forefront of ecological research ever since. The six research stations of the Institute provide a ready access to sites and to environmental and ecological problems in any part of Britain. In addition to the broad environmental knowledge and experience expected of the modern ecologist, each station has a range of special expertise and facilities. Thus, the Institute is able to provide unparallelled opportunities for long-term, multidisciplinary studies of complex environmental and ecological problems.

ITE undertakes specialist ecological research on subjects ranging from micro-organisms to trees and mammals, from coastal habitats to uplands, from derelict land to air pollution. Understanding the ecology of different species of natural and man-made communities plays an increasingly important role in areas such as improving productivity in forestry, rehabilitating disturbed sites, monitoring the effects of pollution, managing and conserving wildlife, and controlling pests.

The Institute's research is financed by the UK Government through the science budget, and by private and public sector customers who commission or sponsor specific research programmes. ITE's expertise is also widely used by international organisations in overseas collaborative projects.

The results of ITE research are available to those responsible for the protection, management and wise use of our natural resources, being published in a wide range of scientific journals, and in an ITE series of publications. The Annual Report contains more general information.

A J Gray and P E M Benham
Institute of Terrestrial Ecology
Furzebrook Research Station
Wareham, Dorset
BH20 5AS
Tel: 0929 551518-9

Contents

4   INTRODUCTION

5   *SPARTINA ANGLICA* – THE EVOLUTIONARY AND ECOLOGICAL
     BACKGROUND
     (A J Gray, P E M Benham and A F Raybould)

11   THE CURRENT STATUS OF *SPARTINA ANGLICA* IN BRITAIN
     (K Charman)

15   POPULATION DIFFERENTIATION IN *SPARTINA* IN THE DEE
     ESTUARY – COMMON GARDEN AND RECIPROCAL
     TRANSPLANT EXPERIMENTS
     (M I Hill)

20   THE SEED BIOLOGY OF *SPARTINA ANGLICA*
     (T C Marks and P H Mullins)

26   MORPHOLOGICAL VARIATION AMONG NATURAL
     POPULATIONS OF *SPARTINA ANGLICA*
     (J D Thompson)

34   THE PRIMARY PRODUCTIVITY OF *SPARTINA ANGLICA* ON AN
     EAST ANGLIAN ESTUARY
     (S P Long, R Dunn, D Jackson, S B Othman and M H Yaakub)

39   THE COMPETITIVE ABILITY OF *SPARTINA ANGLICA* ON DUTCH
     SALT MARSHES
     (M Scholten and J Rozema)

48   *SPARTINA* AS A BIOFUEL
     (R Scott, T V Callaghan and G J Lawson)

52   *SPARTINA ANGLICA* AND OIL : SPILL AND EFFLUENT EFFECTS,
     CLEAN-UP AND REHABILITATION
     (J M Baker, J H Oldham, C M Wilson, B Dicks, D I Little and
     D Levell)

63   THE RESPONSE OF *SPARTINA ANGLICA* TO HEAVY METAL
     POLLUTION
     (J Rozema, M L Otte, R Broekman, G Kamber and H Punte)

69   CHANGES IN THE NUMBERS OF DUNLIN (*CALIDRIS ALPINA*) IN
     BRITISH ESTUARIES IN RELATION TO CHANGES IN THE
     ABUNDANCE OF *SPARTINA*
     (J D Goss-Custard and M E Moser)

72   TWENTY-FIVE YEARS OF INTRODUCED *SPARTINA ANGLICA* IN
     CHINA
     (C H Chung)

77   *SPARTINA* – FRIEND OR FOE? A CONSERVATION VIEWPOINT
     (J P Doody)

Introduction

Very close to 100 years ago, an event occurred somewhere along the salt marshes fringing the Solent estuary in southern England which was to have a profound effect on the ecology of intertidal mudflats and marshes throughout the world. A natural doubling of the chromosome complement in the sterile hybrid *Spartina x townsendii* created a vigorous, fertile, amphidiploid plant, *Spartina anglica*, which has spread, both naturally and by deliberate introductions, to dominate the lower zones of many salt marshes in the temperate regions of both hemispheres.

The spectrum of ecological problems which have resulted from the dramatic spread of the species is discussed in this volume by research scientists from a wide range of backgrounds and interests. The chapters are based partly on papers presented at an ITE workshop held at its Furzebrook Research Station in 1985, considerably updated in 1988, and include further invited contributions. They illustrate that what Dr Joyce Lambert dubbed 'the *Spartina* story' (*Nature, Lond.*, **204,** 1136–1138 (1964)) is far from over.

The prospect of continuing coastal change, with rising sea levels and global warming, adds new possibilities for the future of the species. The effect of rising temperatures alone on a plant which may be limited in its primary productivity, seed production and northward spread by temperature-dependent factors provides an intriguing new dimension to the role of *Spartina* in the development of coastal marshes.

Although most contributions cover work on *Spartina* in Great Britain and Europe, we have included a report of the dramatic influence of the grass on the Chinese coast, to which it was introduced only 25 years ago. The provider of that introduced material, Dr Derek Ranwell, who has made such an important contribution to research on the species and who was present at our original workshop, died last year. We should like to dedicate this volume to his memory.

Alan Gray and Paulina Benham

CHAPTER 1

Spartina anglica – the evolutionary and ecological background

A J Gray[1], P E M Benham[1] and A F Raybould[2]

[1] *Institute of Terrestrial Ecology, Furzebrook Research Station, Wareham, Dorset, BH20 5AS*
[2] *Department of Biological Sciences, University of Birmingham, Birmingham, B15 2TT*

Summary

The evolution of *Spartina anglica* is described, with new electrophoretic data confirming its amphidiploid origin from the progenitor species *S. alterniflora* and *S. maritima*. Factors influencing the species' successful establishment and spread include its perennial life history and the existence of a zone of mudflat formerly unoccupied by perennial plants – a vacant niche. A feature of the species' spread has been sudden phases of population expansion, apparently initiated by a single year of seedling establishment. The spread and subsequent decline of *S. anglica* along the south coast has resulted in the immobilisation and later release of extremely large volumes of tide-borne sediments. These events presage continuing ecological and evolutionary change.

1. Introduction

In this paper, we review briefly the evolution of *Spartina anglica* and provide new evidence to confirm its allopolyploid origin. Aspects of the spread, and in some areas the subsequent decline, of the species will be discussed, partly to provide a background to the contributions which follow, but principally to raise what we believe to be important but unanswered questions.

2. Origin and evolution

Spartina anglica (a name which is strictly invalid, but widely accepted, having first appeared in the second edition of C E Hubbard's book in 1968) is frequently described in textbooks as the classic example of a natural amphidiploid. Its origin, by chromosome doubling of the sterile hybrid (now designated *Spartina townsendii*) between the European *S. maritima* and the North American *S. alterniflora*, was largely confirmed by Marchant in the early 1960s (Marchant 1963, 1967, 1968; see also Lambert 1964). The original hybridisation occurred in Southampton Water some time prior to 1870, probably near Hythe, where one of the few remaining extensive populations of the sterile F$_1$ hybrid can be found. The hybrid was first recognised in 1878 by the Groves brothers, who called it *S. townsendii* (initially spelt with only one 'i') (Groves & Groves 1880), having first believed it to be a form of the then common *S. maritima* (Groves & Groves 1879). The amphidiploid may have arisen around 1890, and was present at nearby Lymington in 1892 and the Isle of Wight in 1893 (Hubbard 1957; Goodman *et al.* 1969). The sudden increase in the rate of spread of the species along the south coast at the end of the last century accords with the production of a fertile form able to spread by seed

(Stapf 1913). Marchant's thorough investigation of the morphology and cytology of British material led him to suggest the genomic relationships shown in Figure 1 (Marchant 1968). The presence of backcrossed individuals near Hythe, the discovery of a polyhaploid plant closely resembling the sterile hybrid (a polyhaploid is a functional diploid produced from a polyploid via unfertilised gametes), and pairing behaviour at meiosis all pointed to the amphidiploid origin of *S. anglica*.

Despite this remarkable detective work, some small doubts remain. It has not been possible either to produce a hybrid between the parent species or to induce the sterile F$_1$ hybrid to double its chromosome number. Furthermore, Marchant's discovery of the parental chromosome numbers, 2n=60 and 62, which corrected widely different parental chromosome numbers, 2n=56 and 70 reported by Huskins (1931), raised the possibility of an autotetraploid origin of *S. anglica*. The low number of multivalents at meiosis in *S. anglica* suggests that autopolyploidy is unlikely, both the parents forming mostly ring bivalents and therefore

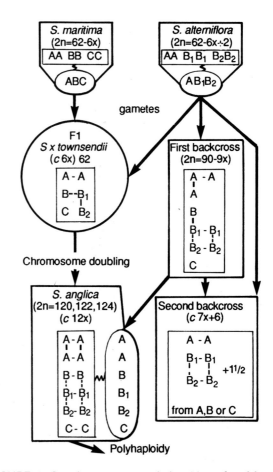

FIGURE 1. Spartina *genome relationships after Marchant (1968)*

being expected to produce an autotetraploid with a high multivalent frequency. As Marchant (1968) admits, however, autotetraploidy remains a possibility. Below, evidence is presented from variation in isoenzyme patterns which demonstrates conclusively the amphidiploid origin of *S. anglica*.

Other unresolved aspects of the evolution of the species remain. These aspects include a possibly polytopic origin – the hybridisation occurring in several different sites. Both the progenitor species were common in the Solent during the last century, where they may have been in contact in the Hythe area for about 70 years. Elsewhere in the estuary, however, *S. maritima* had disappeared by the late 1830s, and *S. alterniflora* was not recorded before about 1816. The progenitor species also occurred together in southwest France, where a sterile plant, later named *S. neyrautii*, was found in 1892, which is believed to be a hybrid from the reciprocal cross (with *S. alterniflora* as ♀) (Arber 1934; Marchant 1977).

Several variants of *Spartina* have been reported, including a dwarf brown form from the Dovey and the Severn estuaries (Chater & Jones 1951), and a densely tillering form from Ireland similar, phenotypically, to *S. maritima* (Boyle 1976). Both these plants have reduced chromosome numbers of 2n=c62 (Marchant 1968; but see Chater 1965) and 2n=56 (Boyle 1976), respectively, and may be polyhaploids. The patches of a densely tillering, sparsely flowering form which can be found in several estuaries, including Poole Harbour, may indicate the widespread production of polyhaploids. Individuals from 17 batches of seedlings collected by Gray from soft mud close to the sea wall at Keyhaven, Hampshire, on 24 July 1984 proved to have chromosome numbers ranging from 2n=54 to 62 (Myers 1985), but, from electrophoretic evidence (see below), were found not to be either of the progenitor species (or, of course, *S. townsendii*, which does not produce seed), but to resemble *S. anglica*. Again, the production of polyhaploids or severe aneuploids is inferred.

The picture is further complicated by the presence in some estuaries of the sterile F_1 hybrid, *S. townsendii*, the existence of which was only discovered by Hubbard in 1956 (Hubbard 1957). Apart from a few south coast sites, it is likely that this primary hybrid was introduced, possibly with *S. anglica*, during the extensive plantings made during the 1920s and 1930s. For example, it can still be found today in Arne Bay, Poole Harbour, an area from which an estimated 175 000 plant fragments were exported between 1924 and 1936 to more than 130 sites around the world (Hubbard 1965). At Arne, *S. townsendii* is now largely confined to a few plants in the upper marsh, indicating that, as is widely believed to have happened elsewhere, it has been replaced by the more vigorous amphidiploid. Drok (1983), working in south-west Holland, was unable to relate morphological, reproductive and cytological features among a large sample of plants which included '*S. townsendii*'-types

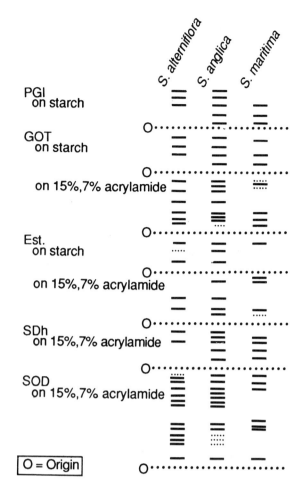

FIGURE 2. *Isoenzyme phenotypes in five enzyme systems for* Spartina alterniflora, S. anglica *and* S. maritima

and both tall and dwarf forms of *S. anglica*. He found some fertile plants which were morphologically and cytologically classifiable as *S. townsendii* and both diploid and tetraploid '*S. anglica*'-type plants in which cytotype was not correlated with size differences.

Several observers have commented on the range of morphological variation in field populations of *S. anglica* (eg Goodman *et al.* 1969; Ranwell 1967; Haynes 1984; Long & Mason 1983), and both Hill and Thompson (pp15 & 26) report significant differentiation between local populations in a range of characters presumably under polygenic control. By contrast, preliminary results of investigations of variation at the isoenzyme level suggest that the amphidiploid is genetically uniform (see below). Several unresolved questions are clearly raised by such findings.

Whatever the genetic base of variation in the species, the success of its establishment and spread has several inseparable elements, not the least of which was pure chance (Gray 1986). It originated from a brief contact between an introduced species and a species at the edge of its range, both of which rarely set seed in Britain and have subsequently decreased in area – *S. alterniflora* to one site only, with the related *S. alterniflora* ssp. *glabra* at three other sites, and *S. maritima* to a few scattered localities from Hampshire to Lincolnshire, with most populations occurring in Essex. Another important element was the perennial nature of the species, enabling the F_1 hybrid to survive until doubling occurred. The many known, and presumed, selective advantages of polyploids over their diploid ancestors (Levin 1983) may have been important, although the ecological implications of increased cell size, later flowering, larger seeds, higher net rates of photosynthesis, greater biochemical diversity through fixed heterozygosity, and other features associated with polyploidy have not been investigated in the *Spartina* complex.

Perhaps the most important element in the rapid expansion of *S. anglica* was the existence of a 'vacant niche' (a philosophically interesting abstraction as its presence is usually only detected when the resources or space it represents have been exploited). Early descriptions and photographs, and observations in recently invaded areas indicate that, in the zone of mudflats below that occupied by perennials, notably *Puccinellia maritima*, and generally above that occupied by *Zostera* species, the only flowering plants found prior to the advent of *S. anglica* were annual *Salicornia* species (and then often thinly scattered). The invasion of that zone and part of the zone to landward, both by natural spread and by widespread introductions, has been well documented (Goodman, Braybrooks & Lambert 1959; Hubbard & Stebbings 1967; Ranwell 1967; Doody 1984), and Charman (p11) reviews the current status of *S. anglica* in Britain.

3. Electrophoretic evidence for the allopolyploid origin of *S. anglica*

When two genomes combine as a result of polyploidy, their affinities can sometimes be detected by electrophoretic separation of isoenzymes (eg Gottlieb 1982). Figure 2 is a diagrammatic representation of the isoenzyme phenotypes observed in five enzyme systems extracted from leaf tissue of British material of *S. alterniflora*, *S. anglica* and *S. maritima*. The methods and full results will be published elsewhere – Figure 2 depicts only the major and reliably detectable bands occurring on starch gels (run at ITE Furzebrook Research Station) or polyacrylamide gels (run at the University of Birmingham) using a horizontal gel electrophoresis procedure (see also Plates 1 & 2). Enzymes were assayed from several British populations of *S. anglica* and *S. maritima* and, with minor exceptions in *S. maritima* and known aneuploids in *S. anglica*, were found to be phenotypically uniform. The single British population of *S. alterniflora*, from Marchwood, is the one shown in Figure 2, North American plants of this species and *S. alterniflora* ssp. *glabra* from Hampshire and Essex showing some minor variation in banding patterns from this plant.

In the five enzymes (and in others not shown here), the phenotype of *S. anglica* (Plate 1 centre) clearly comprises a simple addition of the bands of the two progenitor species. Although complicating factors such as the production of novel hybrid enzymes may occur in

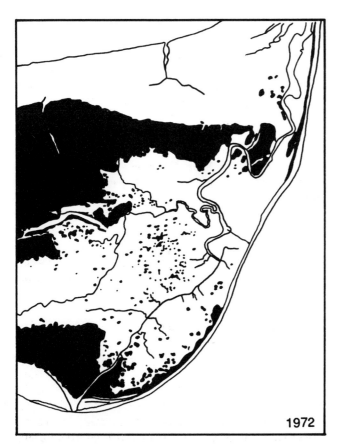

1972

1978

FIGURE 3. *The pattern of invasion and spread of* Spartina anglica *in part of the Conwy estuary, north Wales, between 1972 and 1978. Drawn from aerial photographs at different scales*

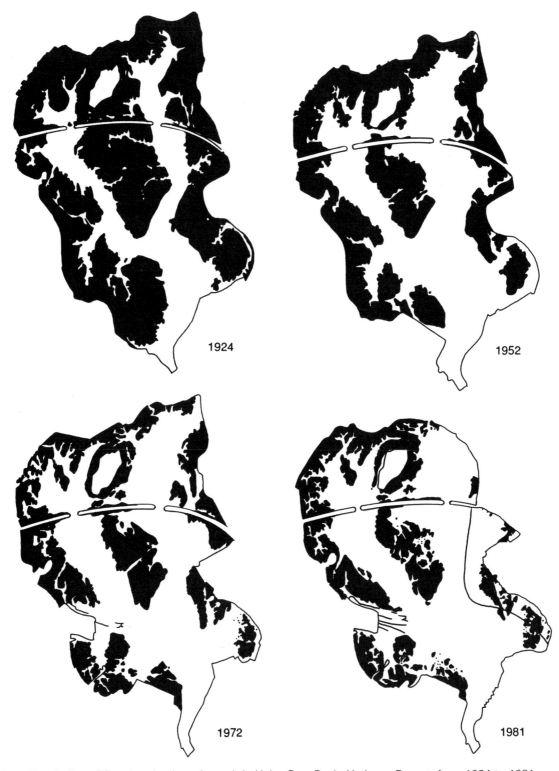

FIGURE 4. *The decline of* Spartina-*dominated marsh in Holes Bay, Poole Harbour, Dorset, from 1924 to 1981 (from Gray & Pearson 1984)*

allopolyploids (Roose & Gottlieb 1976), it is not possible by autopolyploidy to manufacture isoenzymes of markedly different electrophoretic mobility outside the range of mobilities already expressed, as would have to be invoked for both progenitor species in PGI, SDh and Est (on acrylamide), for *S. alterniflora* in GOT (on starch), and for *S. maritima* in Est (on starch). The banding patterns in Figure 2 thus provide unambiguous evidence of the allopolyploid origin of *S. anglica* from the two putative progenitors.

4. Aspects of invasion and decline

Both the rapid spread of *S. anglica* and, in some areas, its subsequent decline have been well charted (see references above and Doody 1984). Here, we consider two aspects of these changes, one relating to the invasive phase, the other to the consequences of widespread regression.

A feature of the invasion of *S. anglica* noted in many estuaries, but not systematically documented, is the

8

sudden rapid expansion of a population which has been established, probably for many years, but has hitherto been growing only slowly. This phenomenon is illustrated in Figure 3, which is drawn from aerial photographs of part of the lower Conwy estuary, west of Llandudno Junction railway station and south of the causeway leading to the Conwy bridges. In 1969, a triangular area of mudflat south of the causeway, bounded on both sides by continuous swards of *S. anglica*, appeared to be devoid of vegetation. By 1972, a large number of almost equal-sized clumps had appeared, and six years later the pattern of clumps was almost identical with few new sites of establishment. The species was introduced to the Conwy in the late 1940s but colonised this area of the estuary following a single burst of (presumed) seedling establishment more than 20 years later.

Similar rapid bursts of colonisation have been noted in several estuaries, including in recent years some of the sites close to the northern limits of the species, eg Morecambe Bay (R Scott pers. comm.) and the Cromarty Firth (Smith 1982). They imply the sudden occurrence of a good year for seedling establishment, perhaps following an infrequent episode of seed production or the arrival at some threshold level in mudflat elevation. Perhaps the phenomenon has a genetic basis – a breakdown in self-incompatibility, for example. The causes of variation in seed production are discussed by Marks & Mullins (p20), and clearly vary considerably in different parts of the species' range. It seems we do not know what constitutes a good year for seedling establishment or the extent to which tide-related phenomena contribute to the sudden expansion of populations which have been 'lurking' for many years.

The widespread dieback of *S. anglica*, particularly in those south coast estuaries where it has been established for more than 80 years, has been widely reported and investigated (eg Goodman 1960; Goodman *et al.* 1959; Goodman & Williams 1961; Haynes & Coulson 1982; Gray & Pearson 1984). The pattern of decline in Holes Bay, Poole Harbour (Figure 4), is typical of that which has occurred elsewhere, although the onset of the decline has varied. For example, it has only recently begun in Milford Haven, south Wales (Baker *et al.*, p60). In Holes Bay, the marshland began to decline in the late 1920s, and by 1981 was, at 80 ha, less than 40% of the 1924 area.

Where such regression of marshland has occurred, there has been a dramatic impact on the sedimentary régime of the seaward mudflats and creeks. Figure 5 shows the percentage changes in the average bed levels of four major channels in Poole Harbour between successive hydrographic surveys from 1849 to 1980. The pattern of change suggests that channels deepened as *S. anglica* spread within the Harbour, presumably removing from circulation extremely large volumes of sediment. Depths above the former *Zostera* mudflat levels of accreted sediment of up to 1.8 m have been recorded below *Spartina* marshes in

Poole Harbour (Hubbard & Stebbings 1968). From the early 1930s onward, the considerable shoaling of all the major navigation channels in the Harbour, including the four in Figure 5, clearly reflects the release of sediment from the eroding marshes (presumably large amounts of nutrients were also released). Some deepening of the most seaward channels has occurred in the past 30 years as gradients steepen and tidal volumes increase. The break-up of the protective *S. anglica* marsh has also exposed the shoreline and islands within the Harbour to wind-generated wave erosion by increased fetch.

The widely accepted explanation of the decline is that, whatever the proximate causes of dieback and death, the process is a 'natural' one, in which *S. anglica* drastically alters the sedimentary and drainage characteristics of the marshlands and paves the way for its own destruction by the creation of anaerobic soils. It is particularly interesting to consider whether this process is cyclic and whether *S. anglica* will reinvade newly accreted sediments in time. There is little evidence of this reinvasion so far, probably because most mudflats to seaward of former *S. anglica* marshes are too low or unstable for the species to colonise. If it does not reinvade, we may expect a gradual reduction of the *S. anglica* niche to one in greater equilibrium with its physical and biotic environment. The evolution of the

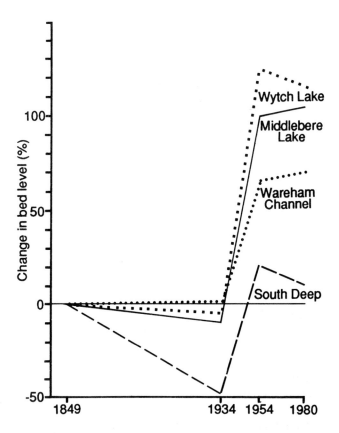

FIGURE 5. *The percentage change in bed levels of four major channels in Poole Harbour, Dorset, between the Admiralty surveys of 1849 and those of 1934, 1954 and 1980. Note the deepening during the expansion of* Spartina *marsh and shallowing during its decline from 1934 onwards*

species is at an early stage, and we are witnessing highly dynamic events. Almost 80 years ago, Stapf wrote:

'The immediate effect of the appearance of this pushful grass on the mudflats of the south coast has been to relieve their bareness and even to beautify them to some extent, and it has no doubt already affected animal life. Physical changes must follow, which, if the grass continues to flourish and spread, will react on the general conditions of the foreshore, resulting probably in the solidification and raising of the mudbanks; but this process will take time . . . Whether the result will in the end be beneficial or to the contrary will depend greatly on local conditions. In any case it will be a change worth watching and studying.'   (Stapf 1908)

His remarkably prophetic words, as the papers in this volume indicate, are no less true today.

5. Acknowledgements

We are grateful to Judith Pearson, Karen Myers and Mick Drury for their assistance, and to Dr Tom Jones (Welsh Plant Breeding Station, Aberystwyth) and Dr David Marshall (University of Birmingham) for their advice on electrophoretic procedures. A F Raybould is in receipt of a research grant from the Natural Environment Research Council.

6. References

Arber, A. 1934. *The Gramineae.* New York: Cambridge University Press.

Boyle, P.J. 1976. *Spartina* M9. A variant *Spartina* in three regions north of Dublin. *Sci. Proc. Roy. Dublin Soc., Ser. A.*, **5**, 415–427.

Chater, E.H. 1965. Ecological aspects of the dwarf brown form of *Spartina* in the Dovey estuary. *J. Ecol.*, **53**, 789–797.

Chater, E.H. & Jones, H. 1951. New forms of *Spartina townsendii* (Groves). *Nature, Lond.*, **168**, 126.

Doody, J.P., ed. 1984. Spartina anglica *in Great Britain.* (Focus on nature conservation no.5.) Attingham: Nature Conservancy Council.

Drok, W.J.A. 1983. Is *Spartina anglica* Hubbard wel een goede sort? *Gorteria*, **11**, 243–252.

Goodman, P.J. 1960. Investigations into die-back in *Spartina townsendii* agg. II. The morphological structure of the Lymington sward. *J. Ecol.*, **48**, 711–724.

Goodman, P.J. & Williams, W.T. 1961. Investigations into die-back in *Spartina townsendii* agg. III. Physiological correlations of die-back. *J. Ecol.*; **49**, 391–398.

Goodman, P.J., Braybrooks, E.M. & Lambert, J.M. 1959. Investigations into die-back in *Spartina townsendii* agg. I. The present status of *Spartina townsendii* in Britain. *J. Ecol.*, **47**, 651–677.

Goodman, P.J., Braybrooks, E.M., Marchant, C.J. & Lambert, J.M. 1969. *Spartina* x *townsendii* H. & J. Groves *sensu lato.* (Biological flora of the British Isles.) *J. Ecol.*, **57**, 298–313.

Gottlieb, L.D. 1982. Conservation and duplication of isoenzymes in plants. *Science, N.Y.*, **216**, 373–380.

Gray, A.J. 1986. Do invading species have definable genetic characteristics? *Phil. Trans. R. Soc. B*, **314**, 655–674.

Gray, A.J. & Pearson, J.M. 1984. *Spartina* marshes in Poole Harbour, Dorset, with particular reference to Holes Bay. In: Spartina anglica *in Great Britain*, edited by J.P. Doody, 11–14. (Focus on nature conservation no.5.) Attingham: Nature Conservancy Council.

Groves, H. & Groves, J. 1879. The *Spartinas* of Southampton Water. *J. Bot.*, **17**, 277.

Groves, H. & Groves, J. 1880. *Spartina townsendii nobis. Rep. bot. Soc. & Exch. Cl. Br. Isl.*, **1**, 37.

Haynes, F.N. 1984. *Spartina* in Langstone Harbour, Hampshire. In: Spartina anglica *in Great Britain*, edited by J.P. Doody, 5–10. (Focus on nature conservation no.5.) Attingham: Nature Conservancy Council.

Haynes, F.N. & Coulson, M.G. 1982. The decline of *Spartina* in Langstone Harbour, Hampshire. *Proc. Hants. Fld Cl. archaeol. Soc.*, **38**, 5–18.

Hubbard, C.E. 1957. In: Report on the British Ecological Society Symposium on *Spartina. J. Ecol.*, **57**, 612–616.

Hubbard, C.E. 1968. *Grasses.* 2nd ed. Harmondsworth: Penguin Books.

Hubbard, J.C.E. 1965. *Spartina* marshes in southern England. VI. Pattern of invasion in Poole Harbour. *J. Ecol.*, **53**, 799–813.

Hubbard, J.C.E. & Stebbings, R.E. 1967. Distribution, dates of origin, and acreage of *Spartina townsendii (s.l.)* marshes in Great Britain. *Proc. bot. Soc. Br. Isl.*, **7**, 1–7.

Hubbard, J.C.E. & Stebbings, R.E. 1968. *Spartina* marshes in southern England. VII. Stratigraphy of the Keysworth marsh, Poole Harbour. *J. Ecol.*, **56**, 707–722.

Huskins, C.L. 1931. The origin of *Spartina townsendii. Genetica*, **12**, 531–538.

Lambert, J.M. 1964. The *Spartina* story. *Nature, Lond.*, **204**, 1136–1138.

Levin, D.A. 1983. Polyploidy and novelty in flowering plants. *Am. Nat.*, **122**, 1–25.

Long, S.P. & Mason, C.F. 1983. *Saltmarsh ecology.* Glasgow: Blackie.

Marchant, C.J. 1963. Corrected chromosome numbers for *Spartina* x *townsendii* and its parent species. *Nature, Lond.*, **199**, 929.

Marchant, C.J. 1967. Evolution in *Spartina* (Gramineae). I. The history and morphology of the genus in Britain. *J. Linn. Soc. (Botany)*, **60**, 1–24.

Marchant, C.J. 1968. Evolution in *Spartina* (Gramineae). II. Chromosomes, basic relationships and the problem of S. x *townsendii* agg. *J. Linn. Soc. (Botany)*, **60**, 381–409.

Marchant, C.J. 1977. Hybrid characteristics in *Spartina* x *neyrautii* Fouc., a taxon rediscovered in northern Spain. *J. Linn. Soc. (Botany)*, **74**, 289–296.

Myers, K. 1985. Spartina *marshes in Poole Harbour, Dorset.* Hatfield Polytechnic/Institute of Terrestrial Ecology. Unpublished.

Ranwell, D.S. 1967. World resources of *Spartina townsendii (sensu lato)* and economic use of *Spartina* marshland. *J. appl. Ecol.*, **4**, 239–256.

Roose, M.L. & Gottlieb, L.D. 1976. Genetic and biochemical consequences of polyploidy in *Tragopogon. Evolution*, **30**, 818–830.

Smith, J.S. 1982. The *Spartina* communities of the Cromarty Firth. *Trans. bot. Soc. Edinb.*, **44**, 27–30.

Stapf, O. 1908. *Spartina townsendii. J. Bot.*, **46**, 76–81.

Stapf, O. 1913. Townsend's grass or ricegrass. *Proc. Bournemouth nat. Sci. Soc.*, **5**, 76–82.

CHAPTER 2

The current status of *Spartina anglica* in Britain

K Charman

Nature Conservancy Council, Northminster House, Peterborough, PE1 1UA

Summary

A comparison of recent information, based on literature searches and some field survey, with that given by Hubbard and Stebbings (1967) reveals a different pattern of change in *Spartina anglica* populations on the east, south and west coasts, respectively. On the east and south coasts, the area of *Spartina* marsh, but not the number of sites at which the species is present, has declined, although the dramatic apparent decline on the east coast may be because of doubtful aerial photograph interpretation. There has been an increase in both the area of *Spartina* and the number of sites on the west coast, although there is considerable between-site variability in the rate and extent of colonisation of *Spartina*. This preliminary survey suggests that *Spartina anglica* occupies almost 10 000 ha in Britain.

1. Introduction

Spartina anglica (sensu lato) is shown in the *Atlas of the British Flora* (Perring & Walters 1976) as being of widespread distribution in both England and Wales, but infrequent north of a line from the Solway to the Firth of Forth. The account of its distribution and abundance given by Hubbard and Stebbings (1967) was derived from a number of published and unpublished sources, a substantial amount of data being obtained from their own interpretation of aerial photographs taken in the early- to mid-1960s. Although *Spartina's* widespread distribution was confirmed, the quantitative data showed major concentrations of the grass in the south coast harbours of Hampshire and Sussex and on the east coast in Essex, north Kent and the Wash embayment. Their paper gives detailed information on the date and type of origin, area and source of information for the component sites of the then known distribution. From the summation of the individual area figures, they derive a value for the total *Spartina* resource of some 12 000 ha.

The major purposes of this paper are:

– to review the current distribution and abundance of *Spartina anglica,* using the best and most up-to-date information available;

– to compare recent survey information for individual sites with that given by Hubbard and Stebbings (1967); and

– to explore some of the relationships between *Spartina* occurrence and abundance with other features of the salt marsh in which they occur.

2. Methods

A number of sources have been used to update the information previously available, as described below.

– The threat of major development proposals at a number of coastal sites has led to detailed mapping of the habitats and communities present, eg the *Wash bunded reservoir scheme* (Randerson 1975), the *Third London airport* (Boorman & Ranwell 1977), the *Severn barrage* (Smith 1979).

– A number of published studies of *Spartina* populations on the south coast (eg Haynes & Coulson 1982; Tubbs 1980) has also included estimates of the area of *Spartina* present.

– My own work has involved sketch-mapping the distribution of salt marsh communities (including *Spartina*) as part of a site-by-site review of the British salt marsh resource. To date, this mapping has concentrated on Wales and the west and south-west coast of England.

There are major practical problems in trying to update the information presented by Hubbard and Stebbings (1967).

i.   The sites for which they give area measurements are not always well defined. For example, although the Severn estuary is divided into a number of blocks, there is no clear indication of boundaries, and therefore detailed comparisons with recent studies are difficult.

ii. In some instances, the changes in *Spartina* area between Hubbard and Stebbings' information and the current data are so great as to call into question their interpretation of aerial photographs. For example, for the Wash they record 1914 ha (based on photographs flown mainly in 1958); in 1971, Randerson (1975) recorded only 207 ha.

iii. Hubbard and Stebbings include no definition of the density or proportion of *Spartina* in a sward which they considered as a qualifying level for inclusion in their data. Although they allude to the problems of mixtures and clumps, no conclusions are drawn. The definition used in this paper is that *Spartina* must dominate a community (ie represent more than 50% cover). Scattered clumps on open mud have been included as a proportion of the total areas covered, or by measurement where clumps are large enough.

3. Results

Despite the problems outlined above, I have used the figures from Hubbard and Stebbings, bringing them up-to-date where possible. The updating has been to a variety of dates, depending on the information available. Where no more recent data are available, Hubbard and Stebbings' original figures have been retained.

Table 1. Area of *Spartina* as given for three areas of Britain by Hubbard and Stebbings (1967), and the updated figures

	East coast	South coast	West coast	Total
Hubbard & Stebbings (1967)				
Area of *Spartina* (ha)	6568	3326	2312	12 205
Number of sites	27	24	35	86
Updated figures				
Area of *Spartina* (ha)	3655	2951	3248	9854
Number of sites	27	29	55	111
(new sites – old sites)	(+1 −1)	(+6 −1)	(+20)	(+27 −2)
Change	44% reduction	11% reduction	40% increase	19% reduction

Table 1 presents Hubbard and Stebbings' original data summarised for the west, south and east coasts of Britain, together with updated figures from the sources outlined above. Hubbard and Stebbings indicated that, in the 1960s, the south coast *Spartina* marshes had passed their earlier growth and invasive phase, and degeneration was both substantial and widespread. More recent changes over the last two decades have been limited to an apparently small reduction in area. In contrast, the decline in stocks on the east coast appears to be very dramatic. The data have been updated on relatively few sites at present (the Wash and a few sites in Essex), and these may be atypical or involve doubtful air photo interpretations. The west coast shows a substantial increase in the quantity of *Spartina* present. The overall pattern outlined above is reflected on individual south, east and west coast sites, although the data in the former two areas are incomplete and additional information might reveal different patterns. The initial and dramatic increase in *Spartina* on the south coast of England, with subsequent planting and invasion of the east and then west coast, could account for the variation in the data presented above, if the species passed through invasive, mature and degenerative phases at each station.

Data from the salt marsh review are currently available for sites on the west coast of England and Wales between south Devon and Morecambe Bay (excluding the Severn estuary – see above). Records are available for a total of 58 salt marsh sites (discrete areas of salt marsh separated from adjacent sites by significant lengths of coastline devoid of salt marsh). Of these sites, 11 contained no *Spartina* and on one additional site none was located, although Hubbard and Stebbings recorded it as present. On 22 sites, the presence of

Spartina noted by Hubbard and Stebbings was confirmed, and on a further 24 sites *Spartina* was found although it had not been recorded in the previous study.

There appears to be a good relationship between the area of *Spartina* found at a site and the size of the whole marsh, with the larger sites containing more *Spartina* (Figure 1). Examination of the size distribution of marsh on

i. sites with no *Spartina*

ii. sites with new *Spartina*, and

iii. existing *Spartina* sites

reveals that it is predominantly the small sites which at present contain no *Spartina* and that the marsh size of sites with known *Spartina* is somewhat larger than that for new sites (Figure 2). Histograms of size distribution for *Spartina* itself show similar trends, with new sites containing smaller quantities of *Spartina* in comparison with known sites (Figure 3). In addition, a shift in size distribution at the same sites with time (Hubbard & Stebbings' data *cf* current data) indicates that, for some sites on the west coast (at least), the *Spartina* population is still expanding.

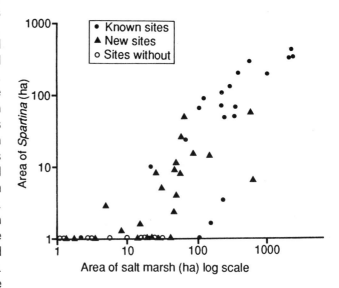

FIGURE 1. Relationship between the area of Spartina *and the area of salt marsh at 58 sites on the west coast of Britain (shown for clarity at base of logarithmic 'y' scale)*

The information presented appears to fit a logical sequence of invasion and growth, starting with the largest sites – presumably with the greatest probability and size of potential *Spartina* habitat for planting or invasion by seed. This simple analysis belies the fact that the percentage area of *Spartina* for each marsh reveals little pattern, when plotted against total area of marsh (Figure 4). Large, medium and small sites all vary widely in the proportion of *Spartina* present. Within the overall increase in *Spartina* resources of the west coast

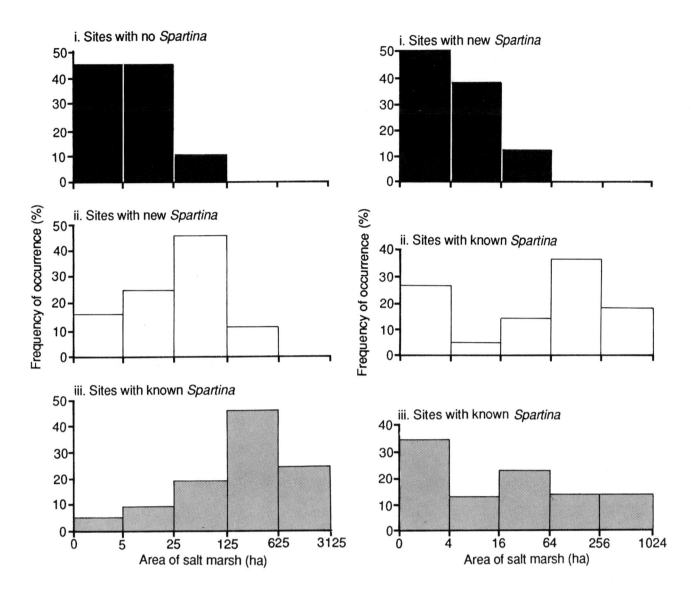

FIGURE 2. Size distribution of salt marsh on 58 sites on the west coast of Britain for sites with (i) no Spartina, (ii) new Spartina, and (iii) known Spartina

FIGURE 3. Size distribution of Spartina on 46 sites on the west coast of Britain for sites with (i) new Spartina, (ii) new Spartina, and (iii) known Spartina (Hubbard & Stebbings 1967)

between the 1950s and the present time, some sites have declining populations of Spartina whilst others are increasing. There is no apparent pattern to this variation in relation to latitude, size of the marsh, or size of the Spartina population.

4. Conclusions

Even when based on an incomplete sample of sites, there seems to have been a marked overall increase in Spartina resources since Hubbard and Stebbings' original survey. However, there is much geographical variation in the response of Spartina populations over the last 30 years. Whilst some of this pattern may be explicable in terms of an invasive sequence, there remains considerable site-to-site variability.

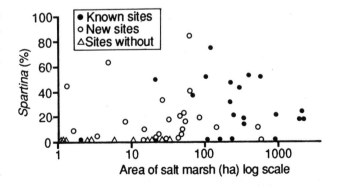

FIGURE 4. Relationship between the percentage of Spartina and the area of salt marsh at 58 sites on the west coast of Britain

5. References

Boorman, L. A. & Ranwell, D.S. 1977. *Ecology of Maplin sands.* Cambridge: Institute of Terrestrial Ecology.

Haynes, F.N. & Coulson, M.G. 1982. The decline of *Spartina* in Langstone Harbour, Hampshire. *Proc, Hamps. Fld Cl. archeol. Soc.,* **38,** 5–18.

Hubbard, J.C.E. & Stebbings, R.E. 1967. Distribution, dates of origin and acreage of *Spartina townsendii* (*s.l.*) marshes in Great Britain. *Proc. bot. Soc. Br. Isl.,* **7,** 1–17.

Perring, F.H. & Walters, S.M., eds. 1976. *Atlas of the British Flora.* London: Botanical Society of the British Isles.

Randerson, P.F. 1975. *The saltmarshes of the Wash. Wash Feasibility Study Ecological Report, Scientific Study D.* Natural Environment Research Council.

Smith, L.P. 1979. *A survey of the saltmarshes in the Severn estuary.* Huntingdon: Nature Conservancy Council.

Tubbs, C.R. 1980. Processes and impacts in the Solent. In: *The Solent estuarine system.* (Series C, no.22.) Swindon: Natural Environment Research Council.

CHAPTER 3

Population differentiation in *Spartina* in the Dee estuary – common garden and reciprocal transplant experiments

M I Hill

Environmental Advisory Unit, University of Liverpool, Merseyside Innovation Centre, 131 Mount Pleasant, Liverpool, L3 5TF

Summary

Common garden experiments in which *Spartina anglica* plants from the Dee estuary were grown in pots in a greenhouse for nine months (experiment 1) and in a sand bed for two years (experiment 2) indicate that there is some ecotypic differentiation between populations from different salt marsh zones. In general, upper marsh plants were taller and had larger leaves and inflorescences than lower marsh plants. Reciprocal transplant experiments established that plants survived and performed better in their home environments, with selection against the alien clones being greater in the upper marsh site than the lower marsh site.

1. Introduction

Despite a considerable literature on the ecology and evolutionary history of *Spartina anglica* in Britain, little is known about the level of genetic variation in natural populations. Variation in field populations has often been commented upon (eg Ranwell 1967; Goodman *et al.* 1969; Long & Mason 1983). Such variation may arise from both ecotypic differentiation and phenotypic plasticity, but their respective contributions are unknown.

The ecological amplitude of *Spartina anglica* is greater than either of its putative parent species in Britain. Ecotypic differentiation is particularly common in species with wide ecological amplitudes (Silander & Antonovics 1979); a species may have expanded its niche by differentiation into distinct adapted populations. Alternatively, it can be argued that, in colonising species such as *Spartina,* a small founder population may have difficulty in maintaining within-population variation, and may respond to a variable environment by phenotypic plasticity (Schmid 1984).

This argument raises a number of important questions.

– To what extent are populations within (or between) marshes genetically differentiated?

– What characters show differentiation?

– Can this variation be demonstrated to be adaptive in the sense of conferring fitness in the local environment?

In this study, these questions are addressed with respect to the *Spartina* populations of different vegetation zones on the Cheshire shore of the Dee estuary salt marshes. *Spartina* was introduced to the Dee estuary in 1928–29, but did not become widely distri-

buted until the 1950s (Marker 1967). The most recent estimate of area of *Spartina*-dominated marsh in the Dee is 526 ha (Deadman 1984). It is now found throughout the zonation, which is unusual in that an extensive *Spartina* sward (zone 2) is found in the upper marsh, separated from the lower marsh *Spartina* communities by a well-drained area (zone 3) of high creek density. The current vegetation zonation, defined by the dominance of *Spartina,* is shown in Table 1.

Table 1. Summary of vegetation zonation of the Parkgate salt marshes on the Cheshire shore of the Dee estuary

Zone	Vegetation
Upper	
1. Shore zone	*Puccinellia – Aster –* upper marsh species *Spartina* in pans and poorly drained sites overlying original course of Parkgate gutter
2. Upper marsh *Spartina* sward	*Spartina*
Middle	
3. Creek zone	*Puccinellia – Halimione – Suaeda – Aster Spartina* in poorly drained areas between creeks
Lower	
4. Lower marsh *Spartina* sward	*Spartina Puccinellia, Suaeda, Aster* and *Salicornia* co-dominant in some areas
5. Pioneer zone	*Spartina* tussocks Localised *Salicornia* pioneer communities and *Suaeda* individuals

2. Common garden experiments

2.1 Methods and results

Common garden experiments – where variation due to environmental factors is minimised – are a well-established method in investigations of population differentiation. Single tillers of *Spartina* were collected from low, middle and upper marsh populations in March 1982, and propagated in a greenhouse for one year.

EXPERIMENT 1

The first experiment was relatively short term, and used clones from lower (zones 4 and 5) and upper (zones 1 and 2) marsh populations, grown in sand-filled pots in an unheated greenhouse. The experiment was conducted as a randomised block design, with three blocks and 30 clones of each population per block. Single tillers were

Table 2. Common garden experiment 1. Population means and F-ratios: results of analyses of variance of characters significant (P < 0.05) at the population level

Character	Population means		F-ratio between populations
	Lower marsh	Upper marsh	
Vegetative tiller number	14.7	12.0	4.164***
Flowering tiller number	3.0	2.1	4.270*
Spike number per inflorescence	2.1	2.5	12.337***
Terminal spike length (cm)	9.1	9.9	3.60*
Vegetative tillers			
Longest leaf length (cm)	13.2	14.2	4.118*
Longest leaf width (mm)	6.0	6.4	5.388*
Third leaf width (mm)	6.0	6.3	6.759*
Flowering tillers			
Tiller height (cm)	38.9	44.8	12.460***
Leaf number per tiller	6.9	7.5	4.921*
Tiller diameter (mm)	4.2	4.6	7.317**
Third leaf length (cm)	15.4	17.1	7.144**
Third leaf width (mm)	6.4	7.0	5.031*

*P < 0.05; **P < 0.01; ***P < 0.001

planted in March and harvested in November 1983, when a range of morphological and dry weight variables was measured.

Analysis of variance showed significant variation at the clone within-population level for 27 out of 35 characters, suggesting considerable clonal variation within the populations sampled. At the population level, 12 variables were significant (Table 2). Lower marsh clones produced more vegetative and flowering tillers than those from the upper marsh. Vegetative and flowering tillers of upper marsh plants were characterised by longer and wider leaves. Flowering tillers of upper marsh clones were also significantly taller, wider at the base, and carried more leaves, longer terminal spikes and more spikes per inflorescence. In summary, these results suggest a trend towards an upper marsh population of more robust, larger biotypes with a lower rate of tillering. There was, however, no significant difference between the populations in the proportion of flowering tillers, or in any dry weight or rhizome character.

Coefficients of variation and variance ratios were calculated to compare the levels of variation in populations for characters which showed a significant population effect in the analysis of variance. These calculations showed no consistent trend over all characters.

EXPERIMENT 2

The second experiment used plants from three populations (lower, middle and upper marsh) which were grown in a sand bed, so allowing relatively unrestricted spread and rhizome production. Plants were grown from single tillers for a period of two years, throughout which time destructive harvests were made. As before, a randomised block design was used, with three blocks and eight clones of each population per block.

As in the first experiment, analysis of variance showed significant differences between populations in a number of characters (Table 3). The most unexpected result was the poor performance and lack of vigour of the middle marsh clones. The middle marsh population mean was significantly lower than at least one of the other two population means in tiller production, most biomass components, the number of shoot complexes (discrete clumps of tillers), the flowering index (date of first flowering), and seed production. In morphological characters (eg leaf length and width, tiller height, spike number), a similar pattern to the first experiment was found. However, less differences were significant and the middle marsh population showed no consistent pattern with respect to the other two populations. In contrast to the first experiment, there was no significant difference between the lower and upper marsh populations in mean tiller number per clone.

Demographic studies of field populations showed that the proportion of overwintering tillers increased, and that of flowering tillers decreased, with elevation (Hill 1984). This pattern was not repeated in sand culture: the proportion of overwintering and flowering tillers was similar in all populations.

2.2 Discussion

The results of these common garden experiments suggest that there is some ecotypic differentiation between *Spartina* populations from different salt marsh zones. This differentiation was most evident in the morphological characters where, in general, upper marsh plants bore taller tillers and larger leaves and inflorescences than lower marsh individuals. This finding can be interpreted as a response to conditions in a relatively mature salt marsh community where the vegetation is taller and forms a dense sward.

Both experiments yielded similar results. However, fewer morphological characters showed evidence of differentiation in the second experiment, possibly because of a carry-over effect from the field environment which persisted in the shorter experiment. Alternatively, because population means in the second experiment were derived from a number of harvests, seasonal variation may have obscured differences between populations. Similarly, the difference in mean tiller number between lower and upper marsh plants, found in the first experiment, was not repeated after two years in sand culture. This finding may indicate a higher initial growth rate in the lower marsh population. The first experiment may also have measured a differential response to density stress in the pot environment, which would not be seen in the sand bed.

The overall lack of vigour of the middle marsh clones in the second experiment is not easy to explain. The distinctive character of this population may reflect the characteristics of the original colonists of this zone (a persistent founder effect), or may result from local

Table 3. Common garden experiment 2. Population means and F-ratios: results of analyses of variance of characters significant (P < 0.05) at the population level

Character	Population means			F-ratio among populations
	Lower	Middle	Upper	
Means over several harvests				
Vegetative tiller number [1]	108(65)[b]	52(41)[a]	96(76)[b]	8.84 **
Total tiller number [1]	142(75)[b]	65(47)[a]	118(87)[b]	11.04 ***
Vegetative dry weight (g) [1]	106(47)[ab]	55(30)[a]	86(58)[b]	4.82 *
Aerial dry weight (g) [1]	122(50)[ab]	62(31)[a]	98(63)[b]	5.40 *
Root dry weight (g) [1]	85(24)[ab]	28(17)[a]	46(29)[b]	4.83 *
Below-ground dry weight (g) [1]	137(44)[ab]	55(30)[a]	89(53)[b]	4.48 *
Total dry weight (g) [1]	261(95)[ab]	118(62)[a]	118(116)[b]	5.01 *
Number of shoot complexes [1]	7.3[b]	4.2[a]	9.0[b]	10.99 ***
Mean internode length (cm)	2.12b	1.78[a]	2.14[b]	4.59 *
Flowering tiller number [1]	28.2(11)[b]	9.8(7)[a]	18(13)[ab]	6.14 **
Flowering dry weight (g) [1]	16(4.2)[b]	7(3.6)[a]	11.6(9)[ab]	7.92 **
Flowering tillers:				
Leaf number per tiller	7.4[a]	8.7[b]	8.3[b]	13.28 **
Third leaf length (cm)	20.0[a]	28.9[b]	25.4[ab]	9.21 *

Values are means of three clones per population at each of six–seven harvests
Values in brackets are means of the first six harvests where a seventh was carried out
[1] Data log-transformed for analysis
Different superscript letters ([a], [b]) denote means that are significantly different (P < 0.05) when tested by the least significant difference
* P < 0.05;   ** P < 0.01;   *** P < 0.001

Character	Population means			F-ratio among populations
	Lower	Middle	Upper	
Means from single harvest of flowering culms				
Flowering tiller number	18.5[a]	9.5[b]	18.1[a]	7.71 *
Flowering dry weight (g)	8.3[ab]	5.0[a]	11.6[b]	7.97 *
Total seed number per clone	964[ab]	580[a]	1341[b]	7.98 *
Flowering index (days)	23.3[a]	46.2[b]	28.4[a]	4.31 *
Spike number per inflorescence	2.6[a]	3.5[b]	3.7[b]	9.98 **
Flowering dry weight per inflorescence (g)	0.44[a]	0.60[b]	0.69[b]	14.79 **
Seed number per inflorescence	48.1[a]	66.8[b]	76.5[b]	15.59 **

Values are means of 30 clones in autumn 1983
Different superscript letters ([a], [b]) denote means that are significantly different (P < 0.05) when tested by the least significant difference
* P < 0.05; ** P < 0.01

differentiation due to inbreeding and a limited input of new genotypes.

There is no evidence in these experiments of a decline in the variability of individual characters during succession, as was found by Gray, Parsell and Scott (1979) for *Puccinellia maritima*, which suggests that the succession is not acting as a 'selective filter', gradually eliminating individuals and reducing variation. Rather, continuous death and recruitment of individuals appears to be occurring throughout the succession.

The monitoring of permanent quadrat sites has demonstrated that the cover and frequency of *Spartina* have declined relatively rapidly since 1980 in zones 3 and 4. Recruitment of seedlings to the population, particularly in zone 3, has also been observed, although their life expectancy was not high. This observation suggests that there is potential for a turnover in the genetic composition of individuals at any one site.

3. Reciprocal transplant experiment

3.1 Methods and results

Common garden experiments can be criticised for failing to expose plants to the conditions which would have been experienced in their natural environment, and which would have been crucial in their evolution. Such experiments can, therefore, only demonstrate the occurrence, but not the significance, of population differentiation. However, using reciprocal transplant experiments, it is possible to gain some understanding of the survival and presumed fitness of individuals in their home and alien sites, and to assess the relative importance of genetically based and/or plastic responses to environmental factors.

The experiment reported here used plants from lower and upper marsh populations transplanted within their own site and into the alien site. Plants were propagated for one year in the greenhouse prior to transplanting, to minimise any carry-over effects, and were planted in the field as single, rooted tillers. At each site, the experimental design was 30 clones from each population replicated over two blocks. The survival and tiller production of the transplants were monitored for 20 months.

Comparison of survivorship using χ^2 contingency tests showed significant differences between survival in home and alien sites on three out of four monitoring dates (September 1983, July 1984 and January 1985)

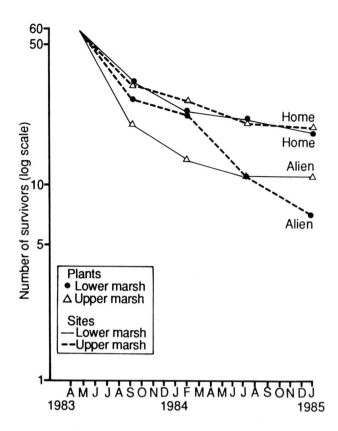

FIGURE 1. Reciprocal transplant experiment. Survival of clones from lower and upper marsh populations transplanted into lower and upper marsh sites

(Figure 1). At the lower marsh site, 30% of home clones survived until the end of the experiment, as opposed to 18% of alien clones. At the upper marsh site, 32% of upper marsh and 12% of lower marsh clones survived. Mean tiller number of surviving transplants was, in general, greater in the home than the alien environment (Figure 2). At the upper marsh site, the difference in the mean tiller number of survivors was significant at all monitoring dates, but greatest in summer/autumn. At the lower marsh site, mean tiller number of home clones was greater than that of alien marsh clones by the end of the experiment (July 1984 and January 1985).

Selection coefficients (Jain & Bradshaw 1966) were calculated to estimate the strength of selection against alien plants at both sites (Table 4). Thus, at the end of the experiment, using survival as a measure, selection was stronger against alien clones in the upper marsh site than against aliens in the lower site. Selection coefficients calculated from tiller numbers over the same period were the same at both sites. At the first monitoring, coefficients calculated from survival data showed stronger selection at the lower marsh site, presumably reflecting differences between the two populations in their ability to avoid uprooting and become established. However, for tiller production in the first summer, the reverse applied: the difference in performance of the two populations was less at the lower marsh site.

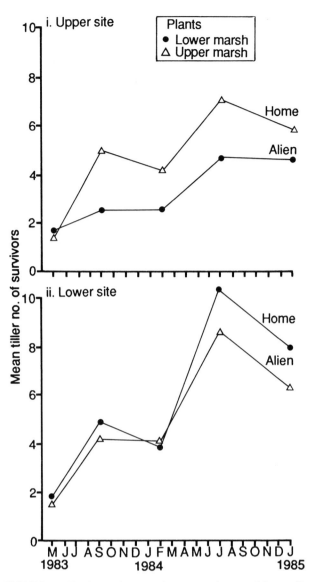

FIGURE 2. Reciprocal transplant experiment. Mean tiller number of surviving clones in upper and lower marsh sites

Table 4. Selection coefficients against alien clones in lower and upper marsh sites, calculated from survival and tiller production data

$$\text{Selection coefficient} = 1 - \frac{\text{performance of alien clones}}{\text{performance of home clones}}$$

		Selection coefficent against aliens	
Date	Character	Lower marsh	Upper marsh
September 1983	Survival	0.39	0.16
	Tiller production	0.13	0.49
January 1985	Survival	0.39	0.63
	Tiller production	0.21	0.21

3.2 Discussion

This experiment demonstrated a greater survival and performance of plants from the home than the alien environment in both lower and upper marsh sites. This finding suggests that there are differences between the populations which are 'ecologically relevant, affecting fitness attributes' (Harper 1982). There is unlikely to be a simple adaptive explanation for these differences: many characters may be important, such as the degree of tolerance to salinity and waterlogging, resistance to erosion, and the form of the whole plant. 'Adaptive story telling' (Gould & Lewontin 1979) is best avoided without a clear demonstration of the adaptive nature of a particular trait.

Further reciprocal transplant experiments would clearly be useful, using plants from more populations at different stages of salt marsh development, and assessing components of their fitness in more detail. This study has demonstrated that genetic differentiation has occurred between some *Spartina* populations on the Dee estuary, and that this aspect of the ecology of the species merits further study.

4. References

Deadman, A.D. 1984. Recent history of *Spartina* in north-west England and north Wales. In: Spartina anglica *in Great Britain*, edited by J.P. Doody, 22–24. (Focus on nature conservation no.5.) Attingham: Nature Conservancy Council.

Goodman, P.J., Braybrooks, E.M., Marchant, J.C. & Lambert, J.M. 1969. Biological flora of the British Isles. *Spartina* x *townsendii* H. & J. Groves *sensu lato. J. Ecol.*, **57,** 298–313.

Gould, S.J. & Lewontin, R.C. 1979. Spandrels of San-Marco and the Panglossian paradigm – a critique of the adaptionist program. *Proc. R. Soc. B*, **205,** 581–598.

Gray, A.J., Parsell, R.J. & Scott, R. 1979. The genetic structure of plant populations in relation to the development of salt marshes. In: *Ecological processes in coastal environments*, edited by R.L. Jefferies & A.J. Davy, 43–64. Oxford: Blackwell Scientific.

Harper, J.L. 1982. After description. In: *The plant community as a working mechanism*, edited by E.I. Newman, 11–26. Oxford: Blackwell Scientific.

Hill, M.I. 1984. Population studies on the Dee estuary. In: Spartina anglica *in Great Britain*, edited by J.P. Doody, 53–58. (Focus on nature conservation no. 5.) Attingham: Nature Conservancy Council.

Jain, S.K. & Bradshaw, A.D. 1966. Evolutionary divergence among adjacent plant populations. I. The evidence and its theoretical analysis. *Heredity*, **21,** 407–441.

Long, S.P. & Mason, C.F. 1983. *Saltmarsh ecology*. Glasgow: Blackie.

Marker, M.E. 1967. The Dee estuary: its progressive silting and salt marsh development. *Trans. Inst. Br. Geogr.*, **41,** 65–71.

Ranwell, D.S. 1967. World resources of *Spartina townsendii* (*sensu lato*) and economic use of *Spartina* marshland. *J. appl. Ecol.*, **4,** 239–256.

Schmid, B. 1984. Niche width and variation within and between populations in a colonising species (*Carex flava* group). *Oecologia*, **63,** 1–6.

Silander, J.A. & Antonovics, J. 1979. The genetic basis of ecological amplitude of *Spartina patens*. I. Morphometric and physiological traits. *Evolution*, **33,** 1114–1127.

CHAPTER 4

The seed biology of *Spartina anglica*

T C Marks and P H Mullins

School of Natural Sciences, Liverpool Polytechnic, Byrom Street, Liverpool, L3 3AF

Summary

Variation in shoot height, inflorescence size, and the proportion of seed-filled spikelets was measured at five British salt marshes. The data suggested that most variation between upper and lower marsh sites occurred on marshes with a large tidal range, and in particular that seed set was reduced in the upper zones of such marshes. Studies of seed production in the Ribble estuary show that pollen fertility is high across all zones, and that the production of filled spikelets is closely related to the date of inflorescence emergence (those emerging after August failing to produce seed). Depressed soil temperatures may be one of several factors, including hypersalinity, causing delayed flowering in the mature marsh.

1. Introduction

The salt marshes of the southern Ribble estuary support extensive *Spartina anglica* swards in a belt varying from 300 m to 750 m in width along their developing seaward margins (Robinson 1984). The marshes have a north-west aspect and are exposed to westerly winds having a 130 mile fetch. The mean spring tide range of 7.9 m, coupled with a very shallow gradient (0.1–0.07%), allows the extensive development of areas of *S. anglica*. Distinct zones of growth are recognisable by their shoot density and vegetation vigour. These zones provide a good opportunity to sample zonal differences which, in a more steeply graded marsh, may be condensed into a narrow strip of vegetation. The rapid rate of marsh development, low

Table 1. Descriptions of the British salt marshes sampled

Marsh	Year	National grid reference	Marsh type and tidal range (m) MHWS–MWLS	Marsh area	Description of areas sampled within marshes
Keysworth, Poole Harbour, Dorset	1980	SY 956 895	Enclosed	Edge	A more or less monospecific stand of *Spartina* growing on the northern edge of the peninsula
			1.7	Centre	A mixed *Spartina*- and *Aster tripolium*-dominated sward in the middle of the Keysworth peninsula
Seafield, Stour estuary, Suffolk	1980	TM 119 332	Enclosed	Lower	The lowest part of the salt marsh consisting of *Spartina* clumps within an area of soft mud
			3.9	Upper	A more closed *Spartina* community associated at its highest levels with *Puccinellia maritima*
Kilnsea, Spurn Head, Humberside	1980	TA 418 143	Open	Pioneer	*Spartina* occurred as widely scattered tussocks, usually less than 3 m in diameter, in an area of mud
			6.0	Lower	*Spartina* and *Salicornia* were found as co-dominants in an open sward dissected by numerous small drainage channels
				Upper	The highest level on the marsh. *Spartina* occurred in association with *P. maritima* and *A. tripolium* in a closed sward
Steart, Bridgwater Bay, Somerset	1981	ST 264 457	Open	Lower	*Spartina* and *Salicornia* occurred as co-dominants within an area dissected by deep drainage channels. Possible erosion at front edge of marsh
			11.1	Upper	A more closed community consisting of *Spartina*, *A. tripolium*, *P. maritima* and *Suaeda maritima*, near the landward edge of the marsh
Banks Marsh, Ribble estuary, Lancashire	1979–1982	SD 375 238	Open	Pioneer	*Spartina* occurred as scattered tussocks, usually less than 10 m in diameter in an area of sandy mud
			7.9	Mature	A closed vigorous *Spartina* sward was present, dissected only by occasional creeks and channels

seedling recruitment, and high morphological homogeneity within the zones suggest that variability is probably the result of phenotypic plasticity.

The morphological characteristics of the *S. anglica* in each of four zones has been described previously (Marks & Mullins 1984). Associated with this morphological variation were variations in seed/spikelet production, seed viability and germination characteristics (Marks & Truscott 1985). The most notable feature of this variation was the poor production of viable seeds by the mature zone sward, which has prolific vegetative growth and large inflorescences. Over 90% of the spikelets in the mature zone failed to develop a seed. In contrast, the adjacent transitional (more seaward) zone, which supported shoots of smaller stature with much reduced inflorescences, had a much higher rate of seed filling, exceeding 80% in some years. Germination characteristics of the seeds also differed.

2. *Spartina* variation at other British salt marshes

S. anglica variation was sampled at the end of the 1980 or 1981 growing seasons at four other British salt marshes to test whether they exhibited patterns of morphology and seed production similar to those seen on the Ribble marshes. The salt marshes selected were thought to be representative of those on the west, east and south coasts of Britain. They covered a wide range of tidal régimes and exposure, and all had been the subject of previous investigation by other workers. The marshes are listed in Table 1, with a brief description of areas sampled. Their locations are indicated in Figure 1, and their tidal régimes compared in Figure 2.

2.1 Variation in shoot height

Marshes with a large tidal range – Kilnsea, Steart and Ribble – showed a distinct increase in shoot height in their landward zones, whilst at Keysworth, which had the smallest tidal range of all sites and was well protected, there was almost no difference in shoot stature across the marsh (Figure 3). At Seafield, vegetative shoots from the lower marsh were taller than those from the upper marsh, but flowering shoots were of equal height in both marsh areas.

2.2 Variation in inflorescence size

The pattern of variation in shoot height was very nearly repeated in the data for inflorescence size (Figure 4). The mean length of the inflorescences was similar in the upper and lower zones of Keysworth and Seafield marshes, whereas the upper zones of Kilnsea, Steart and Ribble had significantly larger inflorescences which produced more spikelets than the lower zones.

The data indicated that the lower zones of those marshes which experience a large tidal range produced shoots and inflorescences of limited growth. Only the upper zones of these marshes supported growth comparable with that at Keysworth.

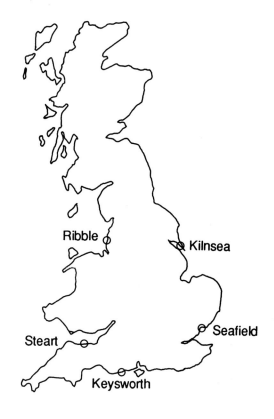

FIGURE 1. *Locations of the salt marshes sampled for zonal variations in morphology and seed production*

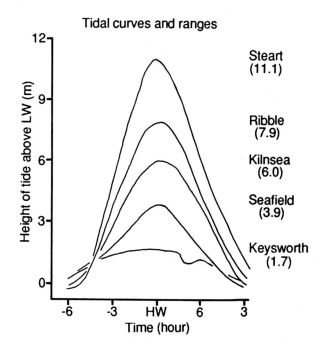

FIGURE 2. *Tidal curves and mean spring tide ranges (m) at the salt marshes sampled for zonal variations in morphology and seed production*

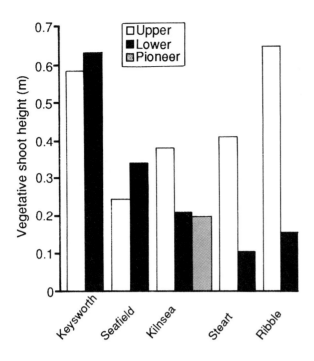

FIGURE 3. *Variation in vegetative shoot height at each salt marsh zone*

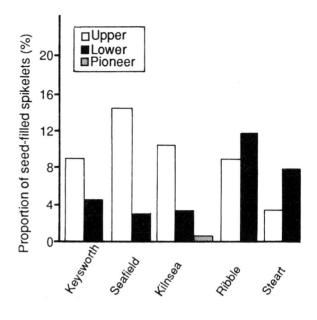

FIGURE 5. *Variation in proportion of seed-filled spikelets at each salt marsh. For letter key, see Figure 3*

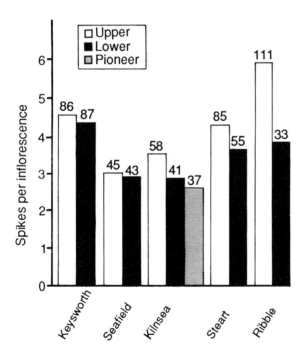

FIGURE 4. *Variation in number of spikes and mean number of spikelets (figures over histograms) per inflorescence at each salt marsh. For letter key, see Figure 3*

2.3 Variation in the proportion of seed-filled spikelets

The only significant differences in seed setting between marsh levels were seen at Kilnsea and Ribble marshes (Figure 5). However, the data suggested a trend from a high proportion of seed setting in the upper

zone of the marshes with a small tidal range to a much-reduced proportion of seed set in the upper areas of those marshes which experienced a large tidal range.

2.4 Discussion

Examination of the temporal patterns of tidal submergence at the Ribble marshes has shown that the upper zones experienced a mean of only 163 tidal submergences per year, and there were several occasions during the growing season when tidal cover was absent for more than 20 consecutive days (Mullins 1985). This finding raises the possibility that saline stress may be implicated in the failure to set seed in the higher zones. Alternatively, the upper and lower populations of *S. anglica* shoots may be genotypically distinct in a similar way to that proposed for high and low marsh populations of *Aster tripolium* (Gray, Parsell & Scott 1979). However, it is difficult to reconcile this mechanism with the apparent speed of marsh development seen on the Ribble marshes (Robinson 1984).

3. Variation in seed quality

3.1 Overall spikelet viability

Spikelets were collected from four zones at Crossens marsh on the Ribble estuary in November, and randomly selected filled and unfilled spikelets were subsequently tested for germination response at 20°C with a 16-hour photoperiod. Spikelets from the invaded zone (most landward) had the highest viability (5.2%, 1 SE=0.43%, n=10) and those from the mature zone had the lowest germination rate (0.6%, 1 SE=1.10%, n=10). Intermediate were those from the pioneer (most seaward) zone (2.8%, 1 SE=1.14%, n=10) and the transitional zone (4.4%, 1 SE=1.45%, n=10). Only the difference between the mature and the invaded zones was statistically significant. In general, the variation in spikelet viability reflected the proportion of filled seeds in each zone, with the exception of the unexpectedly high viability of the invaded zone spikelets.

3.2 Seed germination characteristics

Tests of germination carried out on mature and pioneer zone seeds from the Ribble estuary (Marks & Truscott 1985) revealed the following characteristics.

- Seeds of mature zone plants tended to germinate earlier than those from the pioneer zone.

- Lengthy, low-temperature (5°C) storage promoted germination, but long, high-temperature (15°C) storage delayed it.

- Dry storage delayed germination.

- Germination was inhibited by initial moistening with sea water.

- Germination was more rapid at 20°C than at 10°C.

3.3 Discussion

The exhibited zonal differences in morphological characteristics and reproductive behaviour were also detectable in the quality and characteristics of the seed produced. It was not clear whether the different seed viability and germination characteristics between the mature and pioneer zones were the result of some inherent physiological response or, more simply, whether they reflected a variable such as difference in seed biomass. There is evidence that seed biomass varied between zones (Mullins 1985), but it is not certain that these differences could have accounted for the pattern of seed germination characteristics.

4. Factors causing low seed production

Viable seed production appeared to be relatively poor in *S. anglica*, although the factors responsible are unknown. In other species, seed production is potentially limited by a number of factors, such as the success of pollination, the timing of inflorescence emergence, the degree of ovule abortion, and the availability of resources within the plant.

4.1 Pollen viability

An assessment of the fertility of *S. anglica* pollen was made using aceto-carmine stain. Pollen fertility was high – over 77% – in all zones of the Ribble marsh (Table 2) but no differences were detected between zones. It

appeared unlikely that poor pollen fertility was responsible for the low production of filled spikelets noted in some zones.

4.2 Phenology of shoot development

It was decided to investigate whether phenological differences in inflorescence emergence were related to the final levels of viable seed production within each zone. Individual *S. anglica* shoots were marked in early July and their subsequent development was monitored. Production of filled spikelets was closely related to the date of inflorescence emergence (Mullins & Marks 1987).

Table 3. Percentage of inflorescences setting seed at different dates of emergence

Date	Pioneer	Transitional	Mature
13 August 1981	100	100	100
20 August 1981	100	100	100
26 August 1981	100	100	100
8 September 1981	44	69	38
17 September 1981	—	—	0
25 September 1981	0	17	0
6 October 1981	0	0	0

– no data available

Inflorescences which emerged from their leaf sheaths in August contained some filled spikelets when harvested in November, whereas those which emerged after mid-September contained none (Table 3). A similar relationship was detected in 1980. Moreover, the timing of inflorescence production varied between zones (Figure 6), with only 40% of the mature zone inflorescences emergent by the beginning of September, compared with 62–65% in the transitional and pioneer zones. The late emergence of many mature zone inflorescences, which were then destined to set no seed, could explain, at least in part, the differences in seed production between zones.

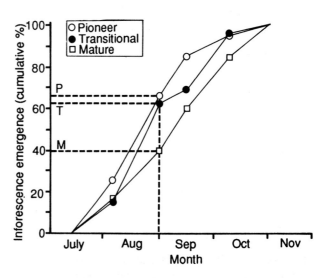

FIGURE 6. The timing of emergence of inflorescences at Ribble salt marsh in 1979

Table 2. Variation in pollen viability between zones. Mean percentage stained pollen ± SE n=5

Sampling date	Pioneer	Transitional	Mature	Invaded
24 August 1981	77.7±7.7	89.5±2.9	91.0±3.4	86.8±1.9
23 September 1981	92.0±1.0	86.2±3.4	92.7±1.3	79.8±8.3

The causes of this temporal variation are not known, but later inflorescence production in the mature zone may have been just one aspect of the slower or later plant growth in this area. Measurements of shoot characteristics across the marsh indicated that peak standing crop and peak shoot heights were attained at a later date in the mature zone compared with the pioneer and transitional zones.

4.3 Soil temperature

It is possible that differences in shoot growth were caused by genetic variation between the *S. anglica* populations in each zone, or by a variety of environmental factors such as soil conditions and patterns of tidal inundation. One such factor selected for further investigation was soil temperature. Measurements were made using the sucrose inversion method (Lee 1969), which provides a measure of mean temperature over an interval of time, and by occasional instantaneous readings with a mercury-in-glass soil thermometer.

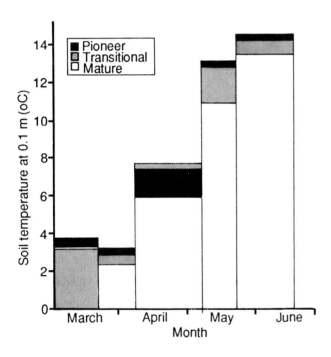

FIGURE 7. *Seasonal trends in soil temperature (0.1 m depth) at Ribble salt marsh in 1982*

Soil temperatures in the mature zone during the spring and early summer were 1–2°C lower than in the more seaward pioneer and transitional zones (Figure 7). It is suggested that depressed soil temperatures in the mature zone were sufficient to delay the development of vegetative shoots and their transition to flowering status.

4.4 Discussion

It appears that, despite prolific vegetative growth, the low production of seed in the mature zone of the Ribble

marshes was not due to the production of inviable pollen. More significant was the delayed development of the aerial shoots in this zone, which reached peak biomass at a significantly later date than those of lower zones. When coupled with the failure of inflorescences emergent after August to produce mature, filled seed, irrespective of the zone of origin, the result was a significant depletion of the proportion of filled seed in the mature zone.

The apparent correlation between late shoot development and depressed soil temperatures in the mature zone invites the speculative suggestion that the factors are causally related. However, also possible, but as yet untested, are mechanisms attributable to other edaphic factors such as salinity and nitrogen availability. Hypersaline conditions could well have developed on the upper areas of this salt marsh during the lengthy periods without tidal submergence, which occurred each summer. Cavalieri and Huang (1981) have concluded that hypersaline conditions may reduce growth of *S. alterniflora* in the USA because of nitrogen deficiency, whilst Jefferies, Davy and Rudmik (1979) suggest that internal competition for nitrogen, induced by saline stress, may lead to a suppression of sexual reproduction in upper marsh populations of perennial species.

The possible failure of some *S. anglica* populations to set seed because of the late production of inflorescences invites a broader interpretation of the fitness of the species for its environment. Long (1983) has explained that, in common with many C4 grasses, *S. anglica* does not commence canopy development until air temperatures exceed 9°C. Because of this fact, the growing season is shortened in comparison with C3 perennial grass species native to north-western Europe. Late flowering may be a further facet of the delayed productive activity in this species, here growing in a temperate climate.

5. References

Cavalieri, A.J. & Huang, A.H.C. 1981. Accumulation of proline and glycinebetaine in *Spartina alterniflora* Loisel. in response to NaCl and nitrogen in the marsh. *Oecologia,* **49,** 224–228.

Gray, A.J., Parsell, R.J. & Scott, R. 1979. The genetic structure of plant populations in relation to the development of salt marshes. In: *Ecological processes in coastal environments,* edited by R.L. Jefferies & A.J. Davy, 43–64. Oxford: Blackwell Scientific.

Jefferies, R.L., Davy, A.J. & Rudmik, T. 1979. The growth strategies of coastal halophytes. In: *Ecological processes in coastal environments,* edited by R.L. Jefferies & A.J. Davy, 243–268. Oxford: Blackwell Scientific.

Lee, R. 1969. Chemical temperature integration. *J. appl. Meteorol.,* **8,** 423–430.

Long, S.P. 1983. C4 photosynthesis at low temperatures. *Pl. Cell Environ.,* **6,** 345–363.

Marks, T.C. & Mullins, P.H. 1984. Population studies on the Ribble estuary. In: Spartina anglica *in Great Britain,* edited by J.P. Doody, 50–52. (Focus on nature conservation no. 5.) Attingham: Nature Conservancy Council.

Marks, T.C. & Truscott, A.J. 1985. Variation in seed production and germination of *Spartina anglica* within a zoned saltmarsh. *J. Ecol.,* **73,** 695–705.

Mullins, P.H. 1985. *The seed biology of* Spartina anglica *(C.E. Hubbard) in the southern Ribble estuary.* PhD thesis, Liverpool Polytechnic.

Mullins, P.H. & Marks, T.C. 1987. Flowering phenology and seed production of *Spartina anglica. J. Ecol.,* **75,** 1037–1048.

Robinson, N.A. 1984. The history of *Spartina* in the Ribble estuary. In: Spartina anglica *in Great Britain,* edited by J.P. Doody, 27–29. (Focus on nature conservation no. 5.) Attingham: Nature Conservancy Council.

CHAPTER 5

Morphological variation among natural populations of *Spartina anglica*

J D Thompson

Department of Environmental and Evolutionary Biology, University of Liverpool, PO Box 147, Liverpool, L69 3BX

Summary

Phenotypic variation was investigated in ten populations of *Spartina anglica,* sampled from the full latitudinal and intertidal distribution of the species in the UK. Sampling and analysis were designed to provide a basis for estimating the relative levels of between- and within-population variation.

Univariate analyses of mean population values showed that plants sampled in complementary zones on different marshes were more similar morphologically than those in different zones on the same or different marsh. Between-population variation was highly significant and accounted for a large proportion of the total variance, suggesting the importance of environmental constraints on growth and the occurrence of a range of phenotypic variants. Multivariate analyses substantiated these trends. The within-population variation accounted for a smaller fraction of the total phenotypic variance, but also showed significant differences. This result, combined with pairwise correlation coefficients, substantiated the observed occurrence of particular morphological forms within several populations.

Comparison with previous work illustrated the temporal consistency of spatial variation in morphology. However, the low levels of seed production recorded contrast with those previously reported, suggesting that seed set may vary considerably with climate. The possibilities are discussed that the variation among these populations has a genetic basis, is due to phenotypic plasticity manifest as a response to environment, or is purely related to age.

'. . . evolutionary ecologists should devote attention not only to the effects of different environments on the average phenotype in a population, but also to their effects on the range and distribution of phenotypes.'

— Begon (1984, p175)

1. Introduction

Spartina anglica has a wide ecological amplitude across different marsh zones and, as a result of introduced plantings and subsequent vigorous vegetative growth, has become widespread around the coast of the UK (Goodman *et al.* 1969; Charman, p11). This rhizomatous, perennial grass occurs as a pioneer of exposed tidal mudflats; as dense, monospecific swards, formed by the rapid growth and coalescence of established tussocks; and as scattered individuals in the mixed salt marsh community in the upper marsh zone.

Different marsh zones can impose markedly different constraints on plant growth (Jefferies, Davy & Rudmik 1979). As a consequence, zonal variation in morphological, demographic and life history traits has been observed in natural and transplanted populations of several species (eg Gray, Parsell & Scott 1979; Gray & Scott 1980; Gray 1985; Jefferies *et al.* 1979, 1981). Several studies on individual marshes in north-west England have reported phenotypic variation for a range of characters in *S. anglica* correlated with changes in elevation (Taylor & Burrows 1968; Marks & Truscott 1985; Hill 1986; Mullins & Marks 1987). Furthermore, such variation may have a genetic component (Hill, p15). However, the possibility that complementary variation may occur in ecologically similar zones of geographically separate marshes, as reported to occur for *Puccinellia maritima* (Gray & Scott 1980; Gray 1985), has not been studied.

In this context, investigations have begun of the genetic and environmental components of the within- and between-population variation displayed by populations of *S. anglica.* In the present study, the results are reported of a morphological survey of ten populations of *Spartina anglica* growing in marsh zones of different successional age and species composition, which encompass the range of its distribution in the UK. The relative contribution of within- and between-population variation to the total phenotypic variation is assessed, and complementary zones are compared.

2. Methods

Ten populations were sampled from marsh zones of differing successional age, species composition, abiotic factors, and latitude during October 1986 (Table 1). For each of these populations, 40–45 randomly selected tillers were carefully unearthed and bagged with any intact tillers and rhizome material. Only 12 samples were collected from the Cromarty Firth population because of its small size. The individual clones were planted into sand-filled 7″ pots in a heated glasshouse at the Liverpool University Botanic Gardens at Ness. During the following month, all flowering culms were measured for a variety of morphological characters (Table 2).

Mean values and coefficients of variation for each character in each population were calculated. Examination of the frequency distribution and log-normal probability plot for each character indicated that, with the exception of SEE and ERG, they had all approximately normal distributions. No significant improve-

Table 1. Sampled population details

Population	Grid reference	
Brands Bay (BB)	SZ 023 846	Old population fringing the most seaward bay in Poole Harbour. Substrate grading from fine organic silts in sheltered part of the bay to coarser sands at the mouth. Extensive stands of *Spartina*, some dieback observed 400 × 10–20 m
Mawddach (MA)	SH 675 187	Swards of *Spartina* fringing a sheltered stretch of the estuary. Fine organic silts 300 × 10–20 m
Afon Menai (AM)	SH 645 732	Young, pioneer population on the mudflats of Traeth Levan 350 × 50 m
Dee pioneer (DP)	SD 270 770	Pioneer population established this decade on exposed, sandy flats. Individual tillers and large tussocks *c* 2 m diameter Two blocks 100 × 100 & 50 × 40 m
Dee sward (DC)	SD 272 772	Dense, monospecific sward adjacent to DP but at higher elevation Two blocks 100 × 30 & 100 × 25 m
Dee mature (DM)	SD 275 775	Scattered tussocks and single tillers in several areas of upper marsh dominated by *Puccinellia maritima*
Ribble pioneer (RP)	SD 360 210	Post-1980 colonisation zone adjacent to the pioneer zone of Marks and Truscott (1985). Sandy flats 100 × 100 m
Ribble sward (RC)	SD 362 212	Very dense, tall sward close to the landward limit of the marsh and a sand-winning works. Outflow of fresh water may be creating low salinity in sediment of black organic silts 200 × 50 m
Ribble mature (RM)	SD 361 211	Represents the 'invaded' zone of Marks and Truscott (1985) 200 × 200 m
Cromarty Firth (CF)	NH 561 602	Population with a central bare patch. Fine, organic sediments. Adjacent to *Phragmites* and *Scirpus* stands 50 × 20 m

Table 2. Morphological characters measured

Character	Abbreviation	Measurement details
Culm height	FCH	Tip of inflorescence to base of culm
Spike number	SPI	Number of spikes
Spikelet number	SPK	Number of mature spikelets
Ergot infestation	ERG	Number of spikelets infested
Seed production	SEE	Number of spikelets that set seed
Culm diameter	CUL	2 cm from the base of the culm
Third leaf length	TLL	Third leaf from top
Third leaf width	TLW	1 cm from the leaf base
Third leaf angle	TLA	Between culm and leaf, above the leaf

ment of their fit to a normal distribution could be made by log or arcsine transformation, so analysis was performed on untransformed data. SEE and ERG were excluded from the analyses because of their highly negative skewed distributions.

Components of variance due to differences between populations, between clones within populations, and within clones (error) were calculated using SAC PROC NESTED (SAS Institute Inc. 1982). The coefficients for the expected mean squares were adjusted for sample size differences, with clones nested as a random factor within populations in a hierarchical analysis of variance (ANOVA) design. The relative levels of significant variation (F-ratios) were determined:

i. between populations, as the population mean square/clone mean square

ii. between clones, as the clone mean square/error mean square.

To examine significant between-population variation further, a SNK multiple range test was used (Winer 1971).

Variation in one character may be determined by its relationship with other characters. Character correlations thus represent an important means of investigating population variation. The degree of correlation among all pairs of characters was calculated for the data set pooled over populations and for each individual population. The overall correlation matrix was subjected to a principal components analysis (PCA), using PROC PRINCOMP, to examine which characters vary interdependently. Finally, to test for any significant joint character variation attributable to differences between the populations, a multiple ANOVA (MANOVA) was employed using PROC GLM.

3. Results

3.1 Individual characters

Univariate ANOVA showed that the variation between populations accounted for a significant proportion of the total phenotypic variation for each of the analysed characters (Figure 1, Table 3), which immediately established the significance of a range of phenotypic variants in different habitats (Figure 2). Significant variation was also demonstrated between clones within the populations (Table 3), but this tended to account for a smaller proportion of the total variation (Figure 1).

Comparison of the mean character values among the populations highlighted the distinctive morphology of the three pioneer populations, AM, DP and RP, which form a statistically similar grouping at the lower end of the range for most characters (Table 3, Figure 2). This finding demonstrated that plants from complementary zones on different marshes were more alike than those from different zones even on the same marsh. The

27

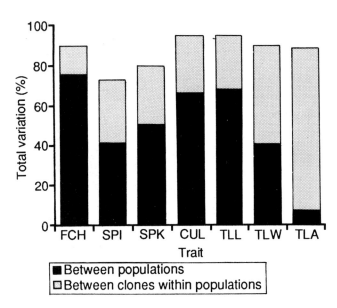

FIGURE 1. *Proportion of the total phenotypic variation in each character attributable to variation within and between populations*

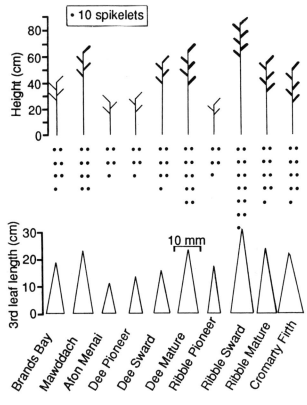

FIGURE 2. *Diagrammatic representation of the morphological variation manifest in ten populations*

Table 3. Results of the univariate statistical analysis of character mean values among the ten populations

| Trait* | Population, mean and significance code letters** | | | | | | | | | | F-ratio significance between | |
											populations	clones
FCH	RP	AM	DP	BB	DC	CF	RM	DM	MA	RC	0.001	0.01
(cm)	24	25	27	40	51	52	54	61	62	85		
	a	a	a	b	c	c	cd	cd	d	e		
SPI	AM	RP	DP	BB	DC	RM	DM	CF	MA	RC	0.001	0.01
	2.5	2.7	2.7	3.5	3.5	4.4	4.8	4.9	4.9	5.7		
	a	a	a	b	b	c	cd	cd	cd	d		
SPK	AM	RP	BP	BB	CD	MA	RM	CF	DM	RC	0.01	0.01
	36	42	47	74	74	77	89	94	101	126		
	a	a	a	b	b	b	b	b	b	c		
CUL	BB	RP	AM	DP	MA	DC	CF	RM	DM	RC	0.001	0.001
(mm)	5.1	5.1	6.1	6.9	8.3	8.5	9.5	9.7	9.7	11.5		
	a	a	ab	b	c	cd	cd	d	d	e		
TLL	AM	DP	RP	DC	BB	CF	DM	RM	MA	RC	0.01	0.01
(cm)	11	14	17	18	19	21	24	24	25	31		
	a	ab	bc	cd	cd	de	e	e	e	f		
TLW	DC	RP	AM	DP	BB	RM	MA	DM	RC	CF	0.001	0.001
(mm)	6.0	6.1	6.4	6.4	6.7	7.7	8.4	8.7	9.1	10.1		
	a	a	a	ab	ab	bc	cd	cd	d	e		
TLA	MA	AM	RP	RM	DM	BB	DP	DC	RC	CF	0.01	0.001
(degrees)	45	47	50	51	52	54	54	55	57	66		
	a	a	a	a	a	ab	ab	ab	ab	b		

* Abbreviations as in Tables 1 and 2

** Populations that do not share a common code letter were found to be significantly (P < 0.05) different in a Tukey–Kramer multiple range test

multiple range tests also indicated that the sward population from the Ribble (RC) had statistically larger mean values for most characters than the other populations. The maximum and minimum values listed in Table 4 provide a clear indication of the protean nature of morphological characters in this species.

Table 4. Minimum and maximum character values and the population of occurrence

Trait	Minimum		Maximum	
	Population	Value	Population	Value
FCH	AM & DP	11.0	RC	118
SPI	Several	1.0	DM	12
SPK	AM	9	DM	285
CUL	RP	3	RC	22
TLL	AM	6	RC	41
TLW	Several	4	DM & CF	14
TLA	Several	30	Several	90

Abbreviations as in Tables 1 and 2

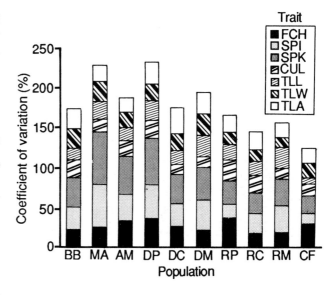

FIGURE 4. Coefficients of variation of individual characters in each population

SEE and ERG were not analysed statistically because of non-normality in the data, but showed similar levels of variation. Seed production was very low. The mean number of seeds per inflorescence varied from zero in the CF and three pioneer populations to 3.3 in the RC population; the remaining populations averaged less than one seed per inflorescence. The percentages of spikelets that set seed showed an identical trend, reaching only 2.6% in the RC population, although one plant did show 13% seed set. For fertile culms only, the percentage of spikelets that set seed was highest in the RM and RC populations, 8% and 10% respectively, compared with less than 5% in the other populations.

Ergot infestation, where the seed is replaced by a mass of fungal tissue as a result of ovary infection by ascospores of *Claviceps purpurea*, showed similar trends. Infection levels were zero in the CF and three pioneer populations, and reached a maximum of 3.5%

of total spikelet numbers in the DM population. The variation in infection between plants was very high; indeed, one inflorescence in the DM population had 20% of its spikelets infected.

The relative amount of character variation, as measured by the coefficient of variation, which takes account of the mean and the unit of measurement, was greater for reproductive characters than for vegetative characters (Figure 3). However, populations showed differing levels of variation depending on the character examined (Figure 4). For instance, DM had a relatively low variation in the CUL but the highest levels of variability in leaf size. The RP and CF populations displayed high amounts of variation in FCH relative to other traits, with noticeably low variability in SPI and SPK, in marked contrast to the pattern of variation in the other populations.

3.2 Character correlations

Calculation of pairwise correlation coefficients between the statistically analysed characters indicated a high degree of statistically significant correlation among all the characters, with the exception of TLA (Table 5). However, with populations treated as sepa-

Table 5. Pairwise correlation coefficients for pooled population data

Trait	FCH	SPI	SPK	CUL	TLL	TLW	TLA*
FCH	–	0.6965	0.7751	0.7607	0.8089	0.5503	0.1772
SPI		–	0.9323	0.6838	0.6652	0.5690	0.1852
SPK			–	0.7076	0.7091	0.5568	0.1711
CUL				–	0.6870	0.5671	0.1908
TLL					–	0.5733	0.1829
TLW						–	0.0446
TLA							–

*Only correlations with TLA were non-significant ($P < 0.05$). Abbreviations as in Table 2

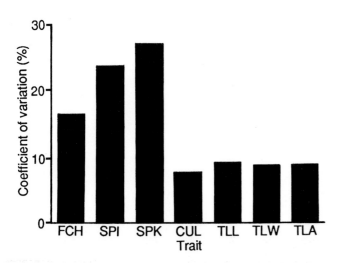

FIGURE 3. Coefficient of variation of each character pooled over populations

rate entities, several non-significant within-population correlations were recorded (Table 6).

The overall correlation matrix was subjected to PCA. It confirmed the significance of the pairwise correlations by their loadings on the first three ordination axes, which accounted for 85% of the variation in the data set. The first two axes described a contrast (or lack of correlation) between TLA and the other characters, and the third axis indicated a contrast in the variability of TLW with that of the remaining characters. In certain clones, an increase in TLW was not correlated with increases in the values for other characters. This result quantifies a trend observed in the field for some of the plants in the pioneer populations to have short culms and short, wide leaves, giving a 'stocky' growth form. By comparison, several plants in the BB, MA, DC and DM populations were observed to have tall culms with long, narrow leaves, giving them a more 'graceful' appearance. The RP and DP populations showed a high degree of correlation for *both* TLL and TLW with the other characters, whereas all the other populations tended only to show significant correlation between *one* of these and the remainder, or no correlation at all (Table 6), providing further indication of the 'stocky' and 'graceful' growth forms. However, a chi-squared analysis of the correlation of TLL and TLW with other characters, employing the Z transformation to normalise the distributions (Zar 1974), demonstrated that these correlation coefficients were not significantly different between the populations.

The low levels of correlation recorded for the CF population (Table 6) are thought to be due to the small sample size, which produced few degrees of freedom in the statistical analysis of the pairwise correlation, and hence decreased the significance of the calculated correlation coefficients. MANOVA further substantiated these character correlation results. A significant proportion ($p < 0.001$) of the character variation could be accounted for by differences between the populations in the joint variation in mean character values.

The character correlations were examined further using bivariate scattergrams for pairs of characters to examine the variation among populations (following Gray et al. 1979). Figure 5 shows the results for FCH plotted against TLL for:

i. the DP and DM populations, and

ii. the RP and RM populations.

This Figure illustrates that the total variation does not decrease in the older populations, and is not contained within that of the younger populations, as demonstrated for *P. maritima* plants grown in collateral cultivation (Gray et al. 1979).

4. Discussion

Different marshes impose different constraints on plant growth (Jefferies et al. 1979). *Spartina anglica* shows a wide range of phenotypic variation in plants collected

Table 6. Significance levels of pairwise character correlations in each population

| Comparison | Population | | | | | | | | | |
	BB	MA	AM	DP	DC	DM	RP	RC	RM	CF
FCH – SPI	***	***	***	***	***	*	***	**	*	***
– SPK	**	***	***	***	***	*	***	***	***	***
– CUL	*	***	***	***	**	***	*	*	**	**
– TLL	***	***	***	***	***	***	*	***	**	*
– TLW					**	*	**	**		
– TLA	**			***						
SPI – SPK	**	***	***	***	***	*	***	**	*	**
– CUL	***	***	***	***	**	*	*	***	**	
– TLL	*	***	***	***			*	*		
– TLW	***	*		***		*	**	*	***	
– TLA										
SPK – CUL	***	***	***	***		*	**	***	***	*
– TLL	*	***	***	***		*	***	***	*	
– TLW	***			**		*	***		***	*
– TLA										
CUL – TLL		***	***	***		*	***	**	***	
– TLW	***	*		***	**	**	***		*	
– TLA										
TLL – TLW	*	**	*	***				***		
– TLA										
TLW– TLA										

* P < 0.05;   **P < 0.01;   ***P < 0.001. Abbreviations as in Tables 1 and 2

i. Dee Pioneer (DP) and Dee Mature (DM) population

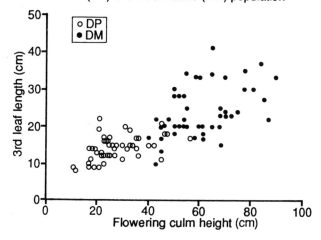

ii. Ribble Pioneer (RP) and Ribble Mature (RM) population

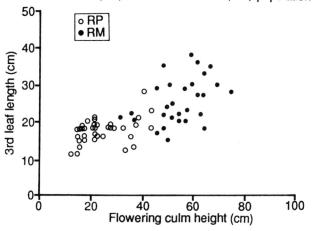

FIGURE 5. *Relative variation in third leaf length and flowering culm height in pioneer and mature populations*

from different zones on a single marsh (Marchant 1967; Ranwell 1972; Marks & Truscott 1985; Hill 1986; Mullins & Marks 1987). The data presented here substantiate the zonal nature of the variation in morphology and the temporal consistency of the patterns described in the previous studies. The similarity of plants from complementary zones on different marshes, and the distinctness of plants in adjacent zones on the same marsh establish the significance of a range of 'phenotypic variants'. This significance is manifest by the small inflorescence size and vegetative stature of the plants sampled in the three pioneer populations (AM, DP and RP), and the trend towards increasing vegetative size and the size and number of flower parts in older zones at higher marsh elevations. In contrast to previous studies on the Dee (Hill 1986) and Ribble (Marks & Truscott 1985) estuaries, seed production was found to be very poor in all zones. This finding exemplifies the variable and often very low

levels of seed production reported for *Spartina anglica* (Goodman *et al.* 1969; Mullins & Marks 1987; Stapf 1914; Taylor 1965). The reason for the low levels of seed set is unclear. *S. anglica* is a C4 grass; hence, seed ripening may be strongly influenced by climate. Consequently, the poor summer of 1986 may have limited seed set. A similar pattern of low seed set following another poor British summer has been observed for populations on the Dee estuary during 1987 (J D Thompson, unpublished data).

Character correlations are a meaningful method of investigating the nature of population variation, in that they may indicate trends that are of ecological and evolutionary significance (Jardine & Edmonds 1974). They have been used to show how the measurement of a limited number of characters can provide a good estimate of variation in a large number of characters in *Puccinellia maritima* (Gray & Scott 1980). In *S. anglica*, the high degree of positive correlation observed between reproductive and vegetative traits reflects the concomitant increase in vegetative stature and inflorescence size observed in natural populations (Marks & Truscott 1985; Hill 1986; Mullins & Marks 1987). At one extreme are the 'giants' of the RC population, at the other end are the 'dwarfs' of the pioneer populations. Such correlations have been described for other species, eg *Verbascum thapsus* (Reinartz 1984) and *S. patens* (Silander 1985). The ecological interpretation is that mature plant height indicates the ability of a plant to obtain light in a sward community, and thus reflects its competitive ability (Givnish 1982) – hence the hypothesis that there has been selection for improved competitive ability in plants collected from the upper marsh zone on the Dee estuary (Hill 1986).

However, the extent to which this zonal variation in morphology is a purely plastic response of a limited number of genotypes to a spatially variable environment, manifest as the plants age, has not been studied. This correlated size increase may represent a decrease in environmental stress with increasing elevation. Pioneer populations exist in conditions where a combination of wave action and salt water inundation severely limit growth and survivorship (Davy & Smith 1985; Hill 1986; J D Thompson, unpublished data). The situation may be exacerbated by the concomitant decrease in nutrient status and the high levels of sulphide that have been reported to limit the growth of *Spartina* spp. on lower marsh sediments (Goodman & Williams 1961; King *et al.* 1982). Furthermore, the interpretation of such correlated size increases must be careful to avoid the bias induced by the simple fact that variation in one character is an 'inevitable biological consequence' of variation in another (Gray & Scott 1980, p105).

'The mean plant is an almost meaningless and biologically misleading abstraction' (Hutchings 1986, p136). In the present study, this description is reflected by the between-clone variation reported in the analyses, which quantify observed variation in stature within the populations. Superimposed on the continuum between 'giants' and 'dwarfs' are two further morphological types. In the pioneer populations, there occurred short plants with short but wide leaves, giving them a robust, 'stocky' growth habit. By comparison, a fourth form could be distinguished in the BB, MA, DC and DM populations that had fairly tall culms with a small number of spikes and long, narrow leaves, imparting a 'graceful' overall stature. This phenotype, which resembles S. townsendii, the sterile hybrid from which S. anglica is derived, has been recorded in a subsequent morphological survey on the Dee estuary and appears to be retained following transplantation to a common garden environment (J D Thompson, unpublished data). It would seem that the variation in size and number of floral parts in S. anglica completely overlaps that shown by S. townsendii.

Reproductive characters frequently show greater levels of variation than vegetative traits (Wilken 1978; Silander 1985). Although this pattern was observed here, the concomitant trend of more significant inter-population differences in reproductive characters, reported in the above studies, did not occur. Floral characters may thus be as plastic as vegetative characters.

The findings that the level of character variation was no greater for pioneer zone populations than for mature zone populations, and that the variation in the latter was not a subset of that for the former contrast with those reported for cultivated populations of Puccinellia maritima (Gray et al. 1979; Gray 1985). The evidence suggests the importance of environmental constraints on growth and the possibility that mature zone populations are not the end result of successional development from an initial founder population similar to that currently found on the pioneer zone.

The description of variation between and within natural populations is a necessary first step towards understanding its causes. The significant inter- and intra-population variation described here, and the variable nature of the character correlations invite the question of whether the variation is based on genetic differences or is a result of environmentally induced plasticity manifest as the plants age. Indeed, such plasticity may have a genetic component (Bradshaw 1965; Jain 1978; Gray 1985); it may serve as a buffer against environmental variation, and thus facilitate the persistence of different genotypes (Schlichting 1986; Sultan 1987). Trials are under way to elucidate the potential importance of these factors to the range and distribution of phenotypes that occasion the levels of population variation presented here.

5. Acknowledgements

My thanks to Tom McNeilly for assistance with plant collection, and Flemming Ulf-Hansen for advice on computing.

6. References

Begon, M. 1984. Density and individual fitness: asymmetric competition. In: *Evolutionary ecology*, edited by B. Shorrocks, 175–194. Oxford: Blackwell Scientific.

Bradshaw, A.D. 1965. Evolutionary significance of phenotypic plasticity in plants. *Adv. Genet.*, **13**, 115–155.

Davy, A.J. & Smith, H. 1985. Population differentiation in the life-history characteristics of saltmarsh annuals. *Vegetatio*, **61**, 117–125.

Givnish, T.J. 1982. On the adaptive significance of leaf height in forest herbs. *Am. Nat.*, **120**, 353–381.

Goodman, P.J. & Williams, W.T. 1961. Investigations into 'die-back' in *Spartina townsendii* agg. III. Physiological correlates of 'die-back'. *J. Ecol.*, **49**, 391–398.

Goodman, P.J., Braybrooks, E.M., Marchant, C.J. & Lambert, J.M. 1969. Biological flora of the British Isles. *Spartina x townsendii* H. & J. Groves *sensu lato*. *J. Ecol.*, **57**, 285–313.

Gray, A.J. 1985. Adaptation in perennial coastal plants – with particular reference to heritable variation in *Puccinellia maritima* and *Ammophila arenaria*. *Vegetatio*, **61**, 179–188.

Gray, A.J. & Scott, R. 1980. A genecological study of *Puccinellia maritima* Huds. (Parl.). I. Variation estimated from single plant samples from British populations. *New Phytol.*, **85**, 89–107.

Gray, A.J., Parsell, R.J. & Scott. R. 1979. The genetic structure of plant populations in relation to the development of salt marshes. In: *Ecological processes in coastal environments*, edited by R.L. Jefferies & A.J. Davy, 43–64. Oxford: Blackwell Scientific.

Hill, M.I. 1986. *Population studies of* Spartina anglica *(C.E. Hubbard) in the Dee estuary.* PhD thesis, University of Liverpool.

Hutchings, M.J. 1986. The structure of plant populations. In: *Plant ecology*, edited by M.J. Crawley, 97–136. Oxford: Blackwell Scientific.

Jain, S.K. 1978. Inheritance of phenotypic plasticity in soft-chess, *Bromus mollis* L. (Gramineae). *Experientia*, **34**, 835–836.

Jardine, N. & Edmonds, J.M. 1974. The use of numerical methods to describe population differentiation. *New Phytol.*, **73**, 1259.

Jefferies, R.L., Davy, A.J. & Rudmik, T. 1979. The growth strategies of coastal halophytes. In: *Ecological processes in coastal environments*, edited by R.L. Jefferies & A.J. Davy, 243–268. Oxford: Blackwell Scientific.

Jefferies, R.L., Davy, A.J. & Rudmik, T. 1981. Population biology of *Salicornia europaea* agg. *J. Ecol.*, **69**, 17–31.

King, G.M., Klug, M.J., Weigert, R.G. & Chalmers, A.G. 1982. Relation of soil water movement and sulphide concentrations to *Spartina alterniflora* production in a Georgia, USA, salt marsh. *Science, N.Y.*, **218**, 61–63.

Marchant, C.J. 1967. Evolution in *Spartina* (Gramineae). I. The history and morphology of the genus in Britain. *J. Linn. Soc. (Botany)*, **60**, 1–24.

Marks, T.C. & Truscott, A.J. 1985. Variation in seed production and germination of *Spartina anglica* within a zoned salt marsh. *J. Ecol.*, **73**, 695–705.

Mullins, P.H. & Marks, T. 1987. Flowering phenology and seed production of *Spartina anglica*. *J. Ecol.*, **74**, 1037–1048.

Ranwell, D.S. 1972. *Ecology of salt marshes and sand dunes.* London: Chapman & Hall.

Reinartz, J.A. 1984. Life history variation of common mullein (*Verbascum thapsus*). II. Plant size, biomass partitioning and morphology. *J. Ecol.*, **72**, 913–925.

SAS Institute Incorporated. 1982. *SAS User's Guide: Statistics.* North Carolina: Cary.

Schlichting, C.D. 1986. The evolution of phenotypic plasticity in plants. *Annu. Rev. Ecol. Syst.*, **17**, 667–693.

Silander, J.A. 1985. The genetic basis of the ecological amplitude of *Spartina patens*. II. Variance and correlation analysis. *Evolution,* **39,** 1034–1052.

Stapf, O. 1914. Townsend's grass or rice grass. *Proc. Bournemouth Nat. Sci. Soc.,* **5,** 76–82.

Sultan, S.E. 1987. Evolutionary implications of phenotypic plasticity in plants. *Evol. Biol.,* **21,** 127–178.

Taylor, M.C. 1965. *The biology of fertile* Spartina townsendii *H. & J. Groves in the Dee estuary, Cheshire, in relation to possible methods of control.* PhD thesis, University of Liverpool.

Taylor, M.C. & Burrows, E.M. 1968. Studies on the biology of *Spartina* in the Dee estuary, Cheshire. *J. Ecol.,* **56,** 795–809.

Wilken, D.H. 1978. Vegetative and floral relationships among western North American populations of *Colomia linearis* Nuttall (Polemoniaceae). *Am. J. Bot.,* **65,** 896–901.

Winer, B.J. 1971. *Statistical principles in experimental design.* 2nd ed. New York: McGraw Hill.

Zar, J.H. 1974. *Biostatistical analysis.* Englewood Cliffs, N.J.: Prentice-Hall.

CHAPTER 6

The primary productivity of *Spartina anglica* on an East Anglian estuary

S P Long, R Dunn[1], D Jackson[2], S B Othman[3] and M H Yaakub[4]

Department of Biology, University of Essex, Colchester, CO4 3SQ
[1] *Present address: Supaturf Products Ltd, Oxney Road, Peterborough, PE1 5YZ*
[2] *Present address: British Nuclear Fuels plc, Sellafield, Seascale, CA20 1PG*
[3] *PO Box 203, Sg. Besi, Serdang, Selangor, Malaysia*
[4] *Present address: Pusat Asasi Sains, University of Malaya, Kuala Lumpur, W. Malaysia*

Summary

This paper summarises field and controlled environment studies of the productivity of *Spartina anglica* from Seafield Bay in the River Stour estuary, Suffolk. The responses of the growth of these plants to variation in temperature, salinity, and availability of nitrogen and phosphorus are described. This information is used in a simple dynamic model to predict the effects that changes in salinity, nitrogen supply and temperature could have on the biomass and productivity of *S. anglica*.

1. Introduction

The *Spartina* marshes of North America have been the subject of several studies of primary productivity; by contrast, those of western Europe have received little attention (Long & Mason 1983). Many of the North American studies have concerned *S. alterniflora,* one of the putative parents of the hybrid from which *S. anglica* is derived. The two species are morphologically similar, and it might be expected that extrapolations could be made from the mass of information on *S. alterniflora.* However, most of the information consists of measurements of above-ground biomass, with few data of below-ground biomass or rate of turnover of the plant organs. Whilst this information provides a detailed picture of the variation in biomass between and within sites, it provides little information on total production or the causes of variation between sites. Thus, we are unable to answer key questions relevant to our scientific understanding and to informed management of *Spartina.* How might variation in production be explained? How productive can we expect *S. anglica* to be at its most northerly locations, and does existing material have the potential to spread further northwards? How might its production in estuaries be influenced by nitrogen pollution or change in salinity resulting from changes in freshwater discharge? Answers to these questions would be possible if we had a reliable model of the responses of production to environmental change.

The basic processes underlying production and standing biomass can be conveniently summarised in a dynamic model of carbon flow (Long & Woolhouse 1979), and this model forms the focus of the studies described here. It has three functions in this work:

i. it provides an ordered framework for examining the completeness of our knowledge of production processes;

ii. it identifies the most important processes and interactions underlying variation in productivity;

iii. it may ultimately allow prediction of responses of production to changes in the environment.

S. anglica is unusually suited among wild plants to predictive modelling – it commonly occurs in quite uniform monotypic stands and has a relatively narrow genetic base. The problems it presents in modelling productivity are therefore similar to those of arable crops. Dynamic models have been widely used to describe the growth of arable crop plants in response to environmental variation (de Wit & Goudriaan 1974). They are appropriate to changing systems, and it is clear from simple observations that *S. anglica* marshes are rarely at steady-state. However, a drawback of these models is that they employ feedback loops in which errors can be amplified. For this reason, it is important that the model is kept simple; otherwise, the tracing of the cause of errors becomes impractical.

Figure 1 illustrates the relational diagram of a model, simplified from Long and Woolhouse (1979). It summarises the factors influencing production and biomass in *S. anglica.* Using even this simplified diagram, we can see that our knowledge of *S. anglica* productivity is very fragmentary. Not only do we lack information on the basic processes determining biomass, ie growth and death rates and their interactions with key environmental factors, but even our knowledge of amount of biomass is limited mainly to measurements above ground. Indeed, most studies which purport to measure the productivity of *Spartina* have, in fact, consisted of biomass and not productivity measurements (Long & Woolhouse 1979; Long & Mason 1983). Productivity, with reference to Figure 1, would be the integral of growth rate, ie the cumulative photosynthetic gain less respiratory losses.

Thus, productivity is the flux of material into the pool labelled biomass in Figure 1, a flux which is partially independent of the amount of biomass present but determined by its rate of turnover, a further factor for which there has been little or no information (Long & Mason 1983). In the context of the relational diagram,

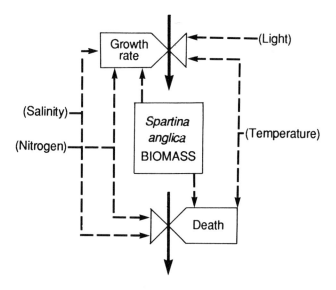

FIGURE 1. *Relational diagram of the dynamics of* Spartina anglica *biomass as determined by the rate variables – growth rate and death rate. Solid lines indicate a flow of carbon, broken lines indicate the influence of biomass and of the driving variables – salinity, temperature, light and nitrogen availability – on the rate variables. The diagram follows the conventions of de Wit and Goudriaan (1974)*

then, our knowledge of *Spartina* productivity is fragmentary. The overall objectives of the studies summarised here were two-fold:

i. to determine the actual gross and net primary productivity of *S. anglica* by combining measurements of change in above- and below-ground biomass with measurements of organ turnover;

ii. to use constants derived from controlled environment studies of the responses of *S. anglica* to the key environmental variables of light, temperature, salinity and nitrogen supply for simulating growth under different environmental conditions.

2. Methods

The study site was an area of 200 m × 50 m within a continuous, monotypic, 30 ha area of *S. anglica* at Seafield Bay on the Stour estuary, south Suffolk (Jackson, Long & Mason 1986). The site was originally bare mudflat; in 1927 planting of *S. anglica* commenced, and by 1950 it had spread to occupy 50 ha. Since then, about 15% of the *S. anglica* has been replaced by *Puccinellia maritima* on the most elevated areas, whilst apparent 'dieback' has removed *S. anglica* from the lowest parts of the marsh. The site is submerged, on average, 570 times per year. The sediment is fine and continuously waterlogged with an oxygen content of 0.3–3.0 mm^3 l^{-1} in the interstitial water. Extractable inorganic phosphorus and exchangeable ammonium levels in the sediment range from 0.1–0.2 mg kg^{-1} and 0.2–0.6 mg kg^{-1}, respectively (Othman 1980; Dunn 1981).

Biomass was determined at monthly intervals by harvesting 20 quadrats of 0.1 m^2 and by simultaneously removing ten soil cores of 30 cm. Samples were located using a randomised block design. Biomass and dead vegetation were separated, leaf area was determined, and all material was dried to constant weight and finally ashed at 550°C to determine an approximate organic content (Dunn 1981; Dunn, Long & Thomas 1981). Turnover of above-ground organs was determined by establishing 20 permanent quadrats in which the development, growth in length, and longevity of leaves and stems were tracked. Changes in weight and losses on death were estimated from weight/length regressions determined each month from the destructive harvests. Turnover of below-ground biomass was estimated as the changes in the weight of dead material between months plus the amount of dead material lost during that interval through decomposition. The relative rate of decomposition was determined with 20 litter bags per month positioned at two depths in the sediment (Roberts, Long & Tieszen 1985).

Primary productivity (P$_n$) for any time interval was estimated using the following equations (Roberts *et al.* 1985):

$$AP_n = \triangle W_s + d$$

where

    AP$_n$ is the above-ground primary productivity (g m^{-2} month^{-1})

    $\triangle$W$_s$ is the change in above-ground biomass

    d   is the amount of biomass lost in the time interval through death

and

$$BP_n = \triangle W_r + \triangle D_r + \bar{D}$$

where

    BP$_n$ is the below-ground primary productivity (g m^{-2} month^{-1})

    $\triangle$W$_r$ is the change in below-ground biomass

    $\triangle\bar{D}_r$ is the change in the amount of dead vegetation below-ground

    $\bar{D}_r$ is the mean quantity of dead vegetation below-ground over the time interval

    r   is the relative rate of decomposition of the dead vegetation below ground over the same time interval.

Simultaneously, plants and seeds were collected from the site for controlled environment gas exchange and growth studies.

3. Results of field measurements of biomass and production

In each year, shoot biomass rose from an April minimum to an autumn maximum (Table 1). On average, 75% of the biomass was below ground, with rhizomes representing roughly half of the total. The peak below-ground biomass was attained in the early winter. Shoot biomass varied significantly between years. The biomass present in September 1980 was almost 50% higher than that in September 1977.

Table 1. Biomass (g m^{-2}) of *Spartina anglica* at Seafield Bay

Date	Leaves	Stems	Roots	Rhizomes
April 1977	10± 2	48± 4	285±15	560±60
June 1977	66± 6	75± 4	165±15	350±40
September 1977	160± 8	186±10	210±20	550±50
December 1977	112± 8	146±10	355±30	625±65
April 1978	25± 5	66± 3	275±20	550±65
April 1979	84± 4	92± 6	–	–
September 1979	213± 8	182±10	–	–
April 1980	100± 5	129±10	–	–
September 1980	216±10	284±12	–	–

From Dunn (1981) and calculated from Jackson *et al.* (1986)

Leaf canopy development was relatively late, being about two months behind the development of the canopy of *Puccinellia maritima* on a nearby north-east Essex marsh (Hussey & Long 1982). In 1977, leaf area index (LAI) rose from a minimum of 0.1 in April to a maximum of just under 2.0 in September. However, significant canopy development did not occur until June, and even by the beginning of July LAI was still less than 1.0. Thus, *S. anglica* at this site will fail to intercept substantial quantities of incoming sunlight during the early summer.

Total production in 1977 (Table 2) was similar to that determined for a *Puccinellia maritima*-dominated salt marsh in Essex (Hussey 1980; Hussey & Long 1982): $AP_n = 810 \text{ g m}^{-2} \text{ yr}^{-1}$ and $BP_n = 610 \text{ g m}^{-2}$. However, production is considerably lower than values reported for the *S. alterniflora*-dominated marshes of North America (Long & Mason 1983). In 1977, approximately 50% of the total production was of below-ground material. By comparison to 1977, above-ground production was similar in 1980, but significantly lower in 1979, illustrating that the marked between-year variability observed in biomass may also be seen in productivity.

Table 2. Primary production (g m^{-2} yr^{-1}) of *Spartina anglica* at Seafield Bay

Year	AP_n	T_s	BP_n	T_r	P_g
1977[1]	700	2.1	650	0.65	4500[3]
1979[2]	474	1.7			
1980[2]	605	2.1			

AP_n = above-ground primary production
T_s = turnover of shoots (AP_n/W_s)
BP_n = below-ground primary production
t_r = turnover of roots and rhizomes (BP_n/W_r)
P_g = gross primary production

[1] Data of Dunn (1981)
[2] Data of Jackson *et al.* (1985)
[3] Determined from gas exchange studies

Gross productivity was some three times net in 1977, suggesting either a high respiratory load, resulting perhaps from the large proportion of biomass below ground, and/or unaccounted losses, such as exudation or leaching of soluble organic material.

Significantly higher biomass levels have been found on *S. anglica* marshes elsewhere in Britain. In October 1978, mean shoot biomass at a salt marsh near Southport was 1145 g m^{-2}, compared to 330 g m^{-2} at Seafield Bay (Dunn *et al.* 1981). Ammonium, the major inorganic source of nitrogen in an anaerobic sediment, has already been noted to be low at this site. Othman (1980) examined the effects of *in situ* N and P fertilisation on five plots at Seafield Bay. Three applications of 5.73 g m^{-2} of ammonium and 4.7 g m^{-2} of phosphate were made in 1978; the results are summarised in Table 3.

Table 3. Effects of N and P fertilisation on above-ground biomass and height of *S. anglica* at Seafield Bay in July 1979

Treatment	C[1]	N	P	N+P	LSD[2]
Biomass (g m^{-2})	84	160	118	208	30
Height (cm)	18	21	24	27	3
LAI	1.1	1.5	1.4	1.9	0.3

Data of Othman (1980)
[1] Control
[2] Least significant difference between treatments (t, $P < 0.05$)

Table 3 shows that the productivity of *S. anglica* at Seafield Bay is limited by both N and P supply. Most significant is the increase in plant height and LAI, which will greatly increase the ability of the canopy to intercept radiation, and thus increase productivity.

4. Controlled environment studies of growth

Effects of temperature, salinity and nitrogen supply on relative growth rates (R) of *S. anglica* collected from Seafield Bay are reported by Dunn (1981), Yaakub (1980) and Othman (1980), respectively. The growth rate of *S. anglica* is approximately zero at 10°C and rises almost linearly to 0.12 d^{-1} for seedlings at 25°C, the rate for mature plants being proportionately less (Dunn 1981; Dunn *et al.* 1987). In response to salinity, R rises by approximately 20% from one milliMolar (1 mM) sodium chloride (NaCl) to an optimum at 86.5 mM NaCl, and then declines steadily almost to zero at 600 mM NaCl, which is roughly equivalent to seawater concentrations (Yaakub 1980). R shows a near-linear increase with the log of ammonium concentration from 10^{-6} M to 10^{-1} M (Othman 1980).

5. Model predictions

Growth parameters determined from the laboratory studies outlined above were used to construct a simple dynamic model of changes in biomass and production of *S. anglica,* based on the relational diagram of Figure 1. The relationships of R at 20°C with biomass, salinity, light and nitrogen were fitted individually to quadratic, cubic, hyperbolic and logarithmic functions, respectively, these functions having previously been chosen as providing the best individual fits. The threshold temperature for growth was assumed to be 10°C, with R increasing linearly with temperature to 25°C. The effects of variation in salinity, biomass and light at temperatures other than 20°C were assumed to be directly proportional to their influence at 20°C. Thus, the coefficient of the relationship of R with temperature was adjusted for other environmental factors in proportion to the known change they produce at 20°C. No account was taken of possible synergistic or antagonistic interactions between these environmental variables in estimating their effects on growth. Daily changes in biomass were calculated from the predicted value of R. Integration of growth rate (R.W) was performed numerically using a second-order Runge–Kutta method (de Wit & Goudriaan 1974). Calculations were performed using programs written in FORTRAN-10 and executed on the University of Essex DEC system-10 computer. The model was tested against controlled environment growth data, showing agreement between observed and predicted values of 10% or better. It was also used to predict change in biomass at Seafield Bay during 1977–78. The model predictions did not differ significantly (t, $P < 0.05$) from observed values between April and October 1977. The model was then used to make tentative predictions of changes which might result from alteration of the environment (Tables 4–6). Daily temperature and light values, recorded during 1977–78 at Seafield Bay (Dunn 1981), were used in these simulations.

Table 4. Predicted effect of salinity change on productivity for S. anglica at Seafield Bay during 1977

Salinity	October biomass (% of observed)
0	48
100	105
200	83
500	32

Table 5. Predicted effect of change in nitrogen supply on biomass of Spartina anglica at Seafield Bay during 1977

Nitrogen	October biomass (% of observed)
1x	94
2x	125
10x	179

The actual salinity of the interstitial water in the sediment water was estimated to vary between 100 mM and 200 mM (Othman 1980). The predictions suggest that any marked increase or decrease in salinity would strongly decrease the amounts of S. anglica present (Table 4). The predicted reduction at 500 mM suggests a negative productivity, and thus the population could not be expected to survive a salinity approaching that of undiluted seawater.

Table 6. Predicted effect of change in temperature on biomass of Spartina anglica at Seafield Bay during 1977

Relative temperature (0°C)[1]	October biomass (% of observed)
−2	38
−1	54
0	94
+1	148
+2	215

[1] In this simulation, 1°C or 2°C was added or subtracted from the recorded temperature for each day of the simulation

From Table 6 it is clear that temperature has perhaps the most profound effect of all on variation in biomass and productivity. A reduction in mean temperature of just 2°C would dramatically decrease autumn biomass and would represent a P_n of about zero. If correct, the simulation suggests that this population of S. anglica is close to the northern limit of its potential range, and that the Hebrides and Udale Bay, the most northerly locations of the species (Long 1983), are probably at the potential limit of northern spread. Productivity of S. anglica would be markedly increased in a year with above-average summer temperatures: a 2°C rise in mean temperature would more than double biomass. This finding may also explain the significantly lower recorded productivities of S. anglica relative to S. alterniflora in North America. Mean summer temperatures at all the North American sites are significantly higher than in southern England. The predicted and unusually strong dependence of S. anglica productivity on temperature is in accordance with its utilisation of C_4 synthesis, S. anglica and its relatives being the only species of significance in the British flora which utilise this form of photosynthetic metabolism (Long 1983).

The study demonstrates that, by combining information on the environmental responses of S. anglica into a dynamic model, we may begin to predict productivity under different environmental conditions and answer the questions raised in the introduction. Clearly, however, more information, particularly of interactions between environmental variables, of genotypic variation, and of the relationships between productivity, rate of spread and survival, will be needed to refine the model as a management tool and to improve understanding of the species.

6. References

Dunn, R. 1981. *The effects of temperature on the photosynthesis, growth and productivity of* Spartina townsendii *(sensu lato) in controlled environments.* PhD thesis, University of Essex, Colchester.

Dunn, R., Long, S.P. & Thomas, S.M. 1981. The effects of temperature on the growth and photosynthesis of the temperate C_4 grass *Spartina townsendii* (sensu lato). In: *Plants and their atmospheric environment*, edited by J. Grace, E.D. Ford & P.G. Jarvis, 303–312. Oxford: Blackwell Scientific.

Dunn, R., Thomas, S.M., Keys, A.J. & Long, S.P. 1987. A comparison of the growth of the C_4 grass *Spartina anglica* with the C_3 grass *Lolium perenne* at different temperatures. *J. exp. Bot.,* **38,** 433–441.

Hussey, A. 1980. *The net primary production of an Essex salt marsh, with particular reference to* Puccinellia maritima. PhD thesis, University of Essex, Colchester.

Hussey, A. & Long, S.P. 1982. Seasonal change in weight of above- and below-ground vegetation and dead plant material in a salt marsh at Colne Point, Essex. *J. Ecol.,* **70,** 757–772.

Jackson, D., Long, S.P. & Mason, C.F. 1986. Net primary production, decomposition and export of *Spartina anglica* on a Suffolk salt-marsh. *J. Ecol.,* **74,** 647–662.

Long, S.P. 1983. C_4 photosynthesis at low temperatures. *Pl. Cell Environ.,* **6,** 345-363.

Long, S.P. & Mason, C.F. 1983. *Saltmarsh ecology.* Glasgow: Blackie.

Long, S.P. & Woolhouse, H.W. 1979. Primary production in *Spartina* marshes. In: *Ecological processes in coastal environments,* edited by R.L. Jefferies & A.J. Davy, 333–352. Oxford: Blackwell Scientific.

Othman, S.B. 1980. *The distribution of salt marsh plants and its relation to edaphic factors with particular reference to* Puccinellia maritima *and* Spartina townsendii. PhD thesis, University of Essex, Colchester.

Roberts, M.J., Long, S.P. & Tieszen, L.L. 1985. Measurement of plant biomass and net primary production. In: *Techniques in bioproductivity and photosynthesis,* edited by J. Coombs, D.O. Hall, S.P. Long & J.M.O. Scurlock, 1–19. 2nd ed. Oxford: Pergamon.

Wit, C.T. de & Goudriaan, J. 1974. *Simulation of ecological processes.* Wageningen: Centre for Agricultural Publishing and Documentation.

Yaakub, M.H. 1980. *Growth, photosynthesis and mineral nutrition of the halophytes* Aster tripolium *and* Spartina x townsendii *in response to salinity.* PhD thesis, University of Essex, Colchester.

CHAPTER 7

The competitive ability of *Spartina anglica* on Dutch salt marshes

M Scholten[1] and J Rozema[2]

[1] *Present address: Laboratory for Applied Marine Research, MT–TNO, PO Box 57, 1700 AB Den Helder, Netherlands*
[2] *Department of Ecology & Ecotoxicology, Biological Laboratory, Free University, PO Box 7161, 1007 MC Amsterdam, Netherlands*

Summary

On the clayey salt marshes in the south-west Netherlands ('delta' area), the inability of *Puccinellia* to compete with *Spartina* leads to the formation of a dense, monospecific *Spartina* sward.

On the silty and sandy salt marshes of the northern Netherlands ('wadden' area), *Puccinellia* is able to replace *Spartina* because of its successful establishment in *Spartina* stands there. The early and rapid seasonal development of *Puccinellia* relative to *Spartina* prevents light from reaching young *Spartina* shoots, and therefore reduces the competitive ability of *Spartina*.

1. Introduction

There are two major salt marsh areas in the Netherlands: the 'delta' area in the south-west and the 'wadden' area in the north (Figure 1). After the introduction of *Spartina anglica* to promote land reclamation in the 1920s, the grass spread vigorously into the lower parts of the salt marshes in the delta area, up till then covered by a Salicornietum and a Spartinetum maritimae vegetation below the mean high water level and a Puccinellietum vegetation above that level (Beeftink 1965). The spread of *Spartina anglica* in the wadden area is of minor importance. Only small, isolated

FIGURE 1. *The two major salt marsh areas in the Netherlands*

tussocks are found within the Salicornietum and the lower Puccinellietum. Development of pure *Spartina* swards is rare here (König 1948; Kamps 1962; Dijkema 1983). *Spartina* is considered to compete for space and light with *Salicornia dolichostachya* and *Puccinellia maritima* (König 1948), and may have a competitive advantage because of its perennial life history and greater height (König 1948).

Several explanations for the difference in the performance of *Spartina* between the two Dutch salt marsh areas have been suggested (Dijkema 1984). *Spartina* is supposed to prefer a poorly drained, soft, clayey soil, brackish conditions and sheltered, tidal waters (König 1948; Chater & Jones 1957; Goodman, Braybrooks & Lambert 1959; Beeftink 1965; Dijkema 1983). These conditions prevail in the delta area (Beeftink 1965). The salt marshes in the wadden area are intensively grazed, making *Spartina* less successful (Dijkema 1983, *cf* Ranwell 1961, 1967). The distribution of plant species across a salt marsh is attributed to spatial variation of environmental conditions (eg salinity, soil texture, redox potential, etc) related to spatial variation in duration and frequency of inundation (Adams 1963; Beeftink 1965; Brereton 1971). The distribution of species depends on their (physiological) tolerance of these conditions (Rozema *et al.* 1985a), and is influenced by interspecific (competitive) interactions (Pielou & Routledge 1976). This paper deals with the effect of interspecific interactions between *Spartina* and *Puccinellia* on the occurrence of *Spartina* in Dutch salt marshes.

2. The status of *Spartina anglica* in the Netherlands

Observations were made on various types of salt marshes in both the delta and the wadden areas (Figure 1). Figure 2 schematically reflects the observed zonation of *Spartina* on those salt marshes, which are classified according to Beeftink (1977).

In the wadden area, salt marsh formation starts about 20–30 cm below the mean high water level with some scattered *Spartina* tussocks. A large population of *Salicornia* is present within and between the tussocks. With the rise in marsh level, the centres of the expanding *Spartina* tussocks are increasingly occupied by *Puccinellia* (Figures 2i, ii). On the silty, wadden-type salt marsh, fused tussocks form 'clumps' (Hubbard 1965). Above mean high water, *Puccinellia* replaces *Spartina* in the open areas of clumps, and at a some-

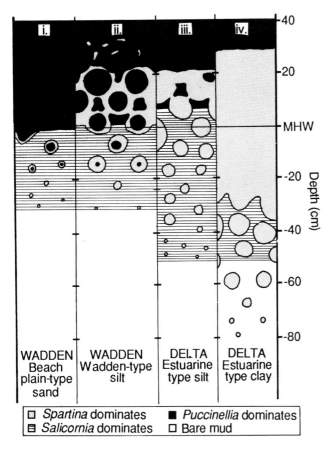

FIGURE 2. *Schematic representation of the zonation of the lower salt marsh on four Dutch salt marsh types*

what higher level is found a *Puccinellia* sward with scattered *Spartina*. There is a gradual transition from a Spartinetum towards a Puccinellietum (Figure 2ii).

On the sandy beach-plain type of salt marsh, the *Spartina* tussocks do not even form clumps because the small, isolated tussocks are rapidly invaded by *Puccinellia*. *Spartina* initiates the formation of small dunes here (Figure 2i). The situation on the clayey estuarine type of salt marsh in the delta area is completely different. *Spartina* tussocks start salt marsh formation more than 70 cm below mean high water. The tussocks grow rapidly without being invaded by other species, thus forming a dense, more or less monospecific sward. *Puccinellia* is confined to an area a few decimetres above mean high water, and there is a sharp transition between the Spartinetum and the Puccinellietum (Figure 2i). On the more sandy delta salt marsh, the scattered *Spartina* tussocks develop within the Salicornietum, and they are not extensively invaded by *Puccinellia*. Around mean high water level, a sparse *Spartina* sward is formed, with *Puccinellia* filling the open space (Figure 2iii).

The field situation can be summarised as follows.

– *Spartina* tussocks are successfully invaded by *Puccinellia* in the wadden area but not in the delta area.

– There is an abrupt transition from the Spartinetum to the Puccinellietum in the delta area and a gradual

transition in the wadden area. In both areas, the transition is more gradual on sandy soils.

– On clayey soils, there is a tendency towards dense *Spartina* sward formation. On silty soils, sparse swards or clumps are formed. On sandy soils, no more than isolated tussocks occur.

Field and glasshouse studies have been undertaken to relate these differences to interactions between *Spartina* and *Puccinellia* under various circumstances. Some preliminary results are discussed below.

3. Field study: a deletion experiment

A method for investigating interspecific interactions in the field removes all individuals of one (or more) species from part of a community where two (or more) species are more or less homogeneously intermingled (Figure 3). Comparing the development of a species in the presence and absence of other species may give an estimate of the interaction between the co-existing species on a particular site (*cf* Allen & Forman 1976; Silander & Antonovics 1982; Fowler 1984). The method can be termed a 'deletion experiment', being the opposite of the 'addition experiment' frequently used in competition research (Spitters 1983).

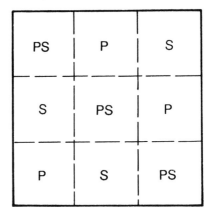

FIGURE 3. *Design of a deletion experiment*
PS = *mixed culture of* Spartina *and* Puccinellia, *no removal*
P = *monoculture of* Puccinellia *from which* Spartina *has been removed*
S = *monoculture of* Spartina *from which* Puccinellia *has been removed*

Two adjacent plots were set out along the edge of a shallow creek within the transition zone from *Spartina* clumps to *Puccinellia* sward on a wadden-type salt marsh on Schiermonnikoog. The plots differed in elevation (*c*4 cm), corresponding with a 15–20 minute difference in the period of tidal submergence, but there were no major differences in salinity, soil texture or redox potential. Shoots were removed early in August 1984. Each plot was divided into nine sections (Figure 3), and *Spartina* was removed from three sections, *Puccinellia* from another three, with the remaining three sections left undisturbed.

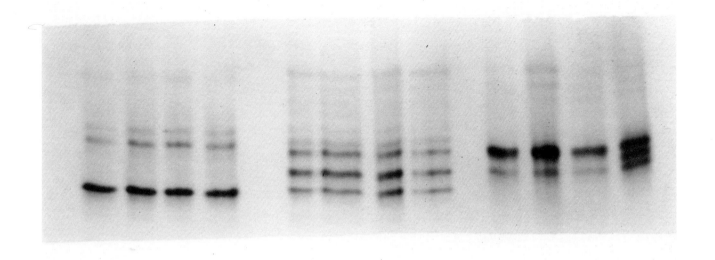

PLATES 1–2   *The origins of* Spartina anglica *revealed by electrophoresis*
1. *Esterase phenotypes in the* S. anglica *complex, (left to right)* S. maritima *(4 individuals),* S. anglica *(2),* S. x townsendii,
S. x neyrautii, S. alterniflora *(3) and* S. glabra *(see Chapter 1) (photograph A F Raybould)*

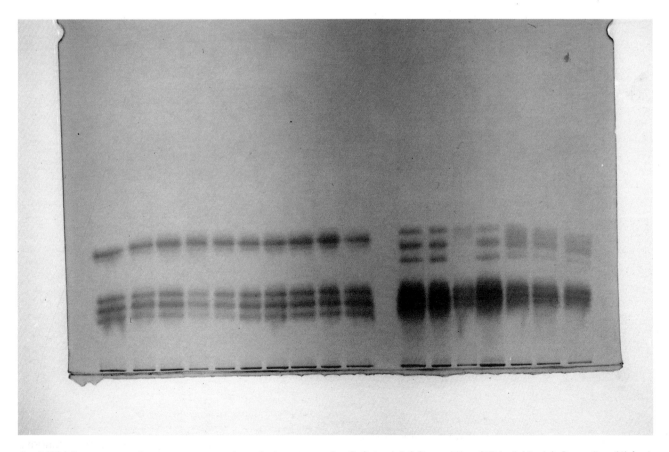

2. *GOT (glutamate oxaloacetate transaminase) phenotypes in: (left to right)* S. maritima *(10 individuals),* S. anglica *(4) and*
S. alterniflora *(3) (see Chapter 1) (photograph A F Raybould)*

PLATE 3. *The possible site of the original hybridisation between* Spartina maritima *and* S. alterniflora *at Hythe, near Southampton, and probably the largest remaining sward of the F1 hybrid,* S. x townsendii *(Chapter 1) (photograph A J Gray)*

PLATE 4. Spartina anglica *plots transformed to* Puccinellia maritima *by cutting in September each year (see Chapter 8) (photograph R Scott)*

PLATE 5.   Seen here being harvested by hand at Southport, Lancashire, Spartina anglica *can yield over 16 tonnes per hectare dry weight of shoots (see Chapter 8) (photograph R Scott)*

PLATE 6.   *Eleven-year-old clones of* Spartina *planted at Fawley to restore a marsh affected by refinery effluent (see Chapter 9) (photograph A J Gray)*

PLATE 7. *Dunlin* (Calidris alpina) (*and ringed plover* (Charadrius hiaticula)) *feeding at the edge of Spartina marsh. The numbers of this wader have declined at a greater rate in estuaries where* Spartina *has expanded most (see Chapter 11) (photograph B Pearson)*

PLATE 8. *Sheep grazing* Spartina *marsh at Qidong marsh, north of the Yangze River mouth, People's Republic of China (see Chapter 12) (photograph M Zhao)*

The plant material removed was used to estimate the above-ground biomass of both species in both plots at the start of the experiment. The plots were harvested after three months (Figure 4). In the higher plot, removal of *Puccinellia* caused a significant increase to *Spartina* biomass (Table 1i), an effect not found in the lower plot. Conversely, the removal of *Spartina* in the lower plot caused a significantly higher biomass production of *Puccinellia*, but not in the higher plot. This finding suggests that the development of *Spartina* is hampered by *Puccinellia* in the higher plot, and that the reverse holds true for the lower plot.

Biomass production in the monocultures hardly differs between plots (Table 1ii). *Spartina* shows a slightly, but insignificantly, higher biomass in the monoculture of the lower zone, *Puccinellia* in the higher one. The difference in biomass production in both plots is much more clear in the mixed cultures (Table 1iii). The *Puccinellia/Spartina* biomass ratio increases more rapidly in the higher plot than in the lower one (Figure 4), indicating a faster replacement of *Spartina* by *Puccinellia*. The re-establishment of *Puccinellia* in sections where it was previously depleted represents the vegetative spread of runners from adjacent sections, and occurs more vigorously in the higher plot. The re-establishment of *Spartina* from underground organs is of minor importance.

Table 1. Biomass ratios found in the deletion experiment

i. Biomass in mixed cultures/biomass in monoculture, at the end of the experiment

	Puccinellia	*Spartina*
High plot	0.76	0.22*
Low plot	0.38*	0.86

ii. Biomass in high plot/biomass in low plot, at the end of the experiment

	Puccinellia	*Spartina*
Monoculture	1.27	0.62
Mixed culture	2.56*	0.16*

iii. Biomass of *Puccinellia*/biomass of *Spartina*, in the mixed cultures

Start of experiment (August)	0.55	6.73
End of experiment (November)	0.16	0.42

* Significantly (P < 0.05) different from 1 (only given for i and ii)

4. A glasshouse study: shoot emergence in spring

In order to measure the effect of interactions between *Puccinellia* and *Spartina* on the spring emergence of shoots, a competition experiment was set up using the replacement series design of de Wit (1960). Hibernating plant parts were collected in January 1985, following a period of extreme frost, from an estuarine salt

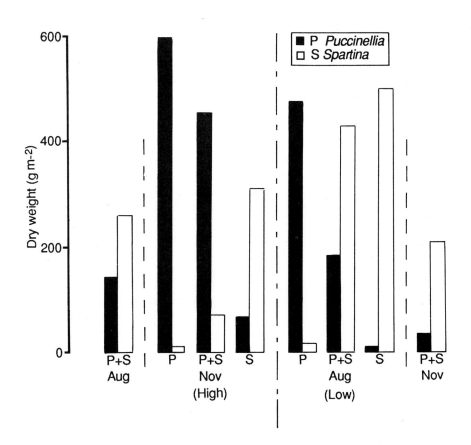

FIGURE 4. *Shoot biomass of* Puccinellia *and* Spartina *at the start of the deletion experiment (Aug) and at the end of the experiment (Nov) in both the higher (high) and lower (low) plots*
P+S = *mixed culture*
P = *monoculture of* Puccinellia
S = *monoculture of* Spartina

marsh near Yerseke. The plant units of the two species were planted in 4500 ml containers in the ratios 15:0, 10:5, 5:10 and 0:15. A unit of *Spartina* consisted of a rhizome section with one well-developed shoot, and a unit of *Puccinellia* consisted of a tuft of 15 tillers. The replacement series was set up for all combinations of three environmental factors, varied at two levels:

i. soil texture: sand *vs* clay (soils collected near Yerseke);

ii. salinity of interstitial water: saline (400 mM sodium chloride (NaCl)) *vs* brackish (200 mM NaCl);

iii. soil moisture: dry (60% water-saturated) *vs* waterlogged (120% water-saturated).

All factorial combinations were duplicated.

The effect of density was estimated by using monocultures of five or ten units of both species. This density series was set up for brackish, dry sand and saline, waterlogged clay, and was also duplicated. The density series is combined with elements of the replacement series to form an addition series (Spitters 1983) (Figure 5).

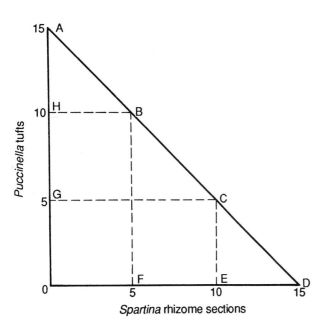

FIGURE 5. *The relationship between the density series of* Spartina *(D, E, F) and* Puccinellia *(A, H, G), a replacement series (A, B, C, D) and an addition series (B/C, H/G and B/C, F/E)*

The effects of nutrition and grazing were investigated by replicating the replacement series on brackish dry sand and saline, waterlogged clay with:

i. the addition of 5 mM potassium nitrate (KNO_3) and 2 mM potassium dihydrogen phosphate (KH_2PO_4) per litre of soil moisture,

ii. clipping all the shoots at a height of 2 cm above the soil surface halfway through the experiment.

Extra monocultures were planted on brackish, dry sand and saline, waterlogged clay, provided with a 3 cm surface layer of dead root mass of the other species. After six and 12 weeks, the growth of five randomly selected units of both species in each container was measured, using the parameters of shoot biomass, number of tillers, and shoot length. Shoot biomass at the first harvest was estimated from total leaf lengths. (Total leaf length was strongly correlated with dry weight: for *Spartina*, 1 m leaf length = 0.50 g dry weight [$r^2=0.98$]; for *Puccinellia*, 1 m leaf length = 0.21 g dry weight [$r^2=0.91$].) The mean relative growth rate (RGR, Causton & Venus 1981) for the first and second six-week periods was calculated from biomass data.

Analyses of variance on the data were used to test the effects of environmental factors on the growth of *Spartina* and *Puccinellia*, and on their interactions, over the total experimental error (Sokal & Rohlf 1981). The results are summarised in Table 2. Figure 6 gives some replacement diagrams.

Under the prevailing experimental conditions, *Puccinellia* seems to be a better competitor than *Spartina* during the initial growth phase. The growth of *Spartina* (RGR and biomass) was reduced when competing with *Puccinellia*, and the reduction was greater on sand than on clay. There seems to be no intraspecific competition between the young *Spartina* individuals – with increasing density.

Puccinellia reached the highest individual tiller numbers at low starting density, especially on sand, indicating intraspecific interaction. Only when tiller density reaches a maximum does further growth take place by elongating individual shoots, indicating light competition (Scholten *et al.* 1987). In mixed cultures with *Spartina*, the growth of *Puccinellia* (RGR, biomass and tiller number) was more vigorous than in monocultures of equal total density, especially on sand. It seemed that *Puccinellia* used the space of the undeveloped *Spartina* to avoid intraspecific competition for light by lateral spread. The shoot length of *Puccinellia* was reduced in mixed cultures and the plants formed a short but dense turf in mixed vegetation with *Spartina*. This turf probably depressed growth of the young *Spartina* shoots in mixed culture, by depriving them of light. The advantage of *Puccinellia* over *Spartina* increased progressively with time, especially on sand (Figure 6). *Spartina* grew (RGR, biomass, length and mean tiller weight) less well on sand than on clay. Growth on clay was better under dry conditions, and on sand under waterlogged conditions. Both drought and saline conditions reduced shoot length and RGR. The growth of *Puccinellia* (RGR, biomass, length, tiller number and mean tiller weight) was less on saline than on brackish soils. Initially, growth was better on sand, but at later stages it was better on clay. Growth was especially retarded on 'dry' sand. There were no measurable effects on the NPK addition, either on individual plants

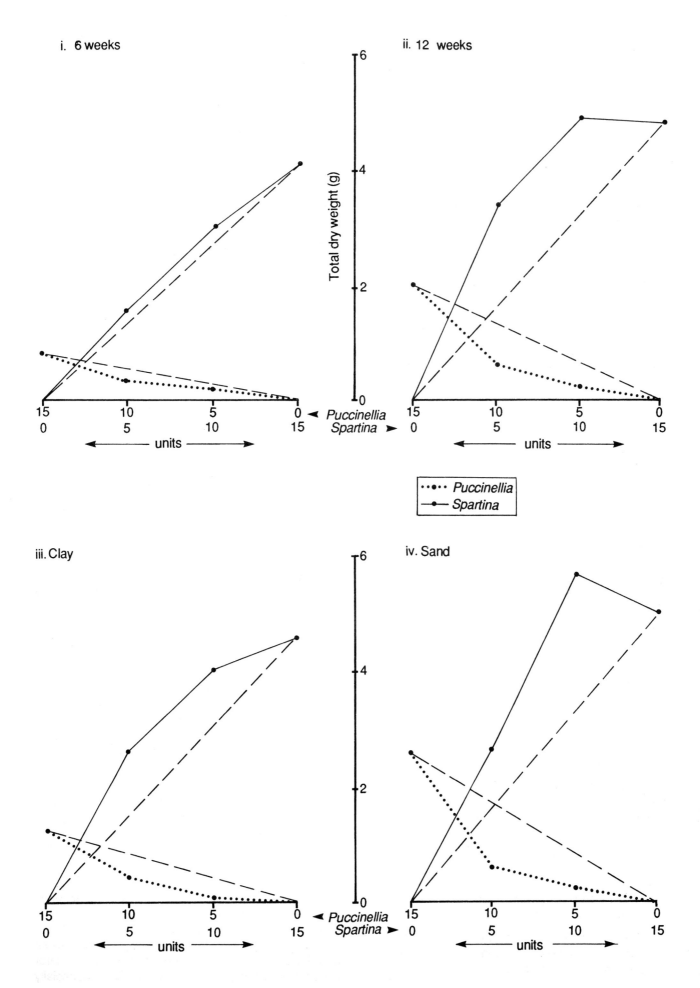

FIGURE 6.   Replacement diagrams of Spartina with Puccinellia; total mean at time 1 (6 weeks, i) and time 2 (12 weeks, ii) and mean at time 2 for growth on clay (iii) or on sand (iv)

Table 2i. Outline of the analysis of variance: the influence of plant interactions and soil characters on growth parameters of *Spartina*

Parameter	Relative growth rate (g g⁻¹ week⁻¹)		Shoot biomass (g)		Tiller number		Shoot length (cm)		Mean tiller weight (g)	
Time of harvest (weeks)	0–6	6–12	6	12	6	12	6	12	6	12
Overall mean	0.22	0.09	0.20	0.37	4.5	4.5	8.9	20.2	0.051	0.076
Least significant difference (P < 0.01)	0.04	0.05	0.10	0.23	0.5	2.2	1.7	4.6	0.019	0.025
Biotic factors										
Competition coefficient	**	***	**	***	*	***	**	***		
Intraspecific competition (Ia) *vs* interspecific competition (Ie)	Ia<Ie	Ia<Ie	Ia<Ie	Ia<Ie	Ia<Ie	Ia<Ie	Ia<Ie	Ia<Ie		
Intraspecific interaction	*	**		*						
Low density (L) *vs* high density (H)	L<H	L<H		L<H						
Interspecific interaction				*						
monoculture (Mo) *vs* mixed culture (Mi)				Mo<Mi						
Abiotic factors										
Soil salinity					*		**		*	
Saline (S) *vs* brackish (B)					S<B		S>B		S>B	
Soil water content		*					*			
'dry' (D) *vs* waterlogged (W)		D<W					D<W			
Soil texture		*		**				**		***
Sandy (S) *vs* clayey (C)		S<C		S<C				S<C		S<C
Interactions										
Comp. coeff. x soil salinity										
Comp. coeff. x water content										*
Comp. coeff. x soil texture				**						

* P = 0.05–0.01;   ** 0.01–0.001;   *** < 0.001

or on intra- and interspecific relations. There seemed to be no competition for nutrients within or between the species. Obviously, under the prevailing conditions, intra- and interspecific interactions were strongly influenced by competition for light and space. Clipping almost completely suppressed the growth of young *Spartina* shoots, whereas *Puccinellia* was less affected, especially on brackish 'dry' sand.

A soil top layer of dead *Puccinellia* roots does not affect the growth of *Spartina*. A layer of *Spartina* root mass, on the other hand, can stimulate the growth of *Puccinellia*, especially on waterlogged clay. Presumably, the better drainage of this top layer facilitates growth of the shallow-rooting *Puccinellia*.

5. Discussion

The establishment and development of *Spartina* populations in Dutch salt marshes are comparable to that described by Hubbard (1965) for Britain. Seedlings give rise to tussocks by vegetative spread, and the forming of clumps or swards by the fusing of spreading tussocks depends on three factors:

i.   the rate of lateral tussock growth,

ii. the maximum shoot density, and

iii. the establishment of other species in the *Spartina* stand.

Rapid lateral tussock growth, a high shoot density, and retarded establishment of other species lead to the formation of a dense, monospecific *Spartina* sward.

Chater and Jones (1957) indicated that tussock spread is greatest on muddy soils, and this can be seen in Dutch salt marshes. It can be related to an easier penetration of rhizomes in soft, wet clay.

Shoot density is said to be reduced in sand and at high salinity levels (Chater & Jones 1957). Caldwell (1957) demonstrated that, as *Spartina* tussocks age, they have a low shoot density in the centre and a high density at the periphery. Interspecific interaction can also reduce shoot density, and, where *Spartina* is able to establish below the mean high water level, it achieves a high shoot density prior to the onset of competition with *Puccinellia* and other species above that level. The lower limit of *Spartina* may depend on tidal amplitude and salinity, the seaward spread being related to duration of immersion (Morley 1972; Hubbard 1969). Reduced immersion leads to the production of more shoots (Groenendijk 1981) and soils below mean high water level are frequently waterlogged, which, at high salinity, reduces *Spartina* growth (van Diggelen 1987).

Table 2ii. Outline of the analysis of variance: the influence of plant interactions and soil characters on growth parameters of *Puccinellia*

Parameter	Relative growth rate ($g\ g^{-1}\ week^{-1}$)		Shoot biomass (g)		Tiller number		Shoot length (cm)		Mean tiller weight (g)	
Time of harvest (weeks)	0–6	6–12	6	12	6	12	6	12	6	12
Overall mean	0.45	0.06	1.46	2.28	31	65	22.0	16.8	0.047	0.036
Least significant difference (P < 0.01)	0.06	0.03	0.32	0.83	6	16	1.6	1.8	0.005	0.006
Biotic factors										
Competition coefficient		***	***	**	***	***	***	**	***	**
Intraspecific competition (Ia) vs interspecific competition (Ie)		Ia>Ie	Ia>Ie	Ia>Ie	Ia>Ie	Ia>Ie	Ia<Ie	Ia<Ie	Ia<Ie	Ia<Ie
Intraspecific interaction		**				*				
Low density (L) vs high density (H)		L<H				L>H				
Interspecific interaction		***		**		**				
monoculture (Mo) vs mixed culture (Mi)		Mo<Mi		Mo<Mi		Mo<Mi				
Abiotic factors										
Soil salinity		***		***	**			***		**
Saline (S) vs brackish (B)		S<B		S<B	S<B			S<B		S<B
Soil water content						**	**			
'dry' (D) vs waterlogged (W)						D<W	D<W			
Soil texture	***	**	***	*	***	*	***			
Sandy (S) vs clayey (C)	S<C	S>C	S<C	S>C	S<C	S<C	S<C			
Interactions										
Comp. coeff. x soil salinity				*				**	*	
Comp. coeff. x water content								*		*
Comp. coeff. x soil texture		**								

* P = 0.05–0.01;   ** 0.01–0.001;   *** < 0.001

The establishment of *Puccinellia* or other species within a *Spartina* stand is facilitated by:

— protection against uprooting by tidal currents. For example, *Puccinellia* reacts to waterlogging by forming lateral roots on the soil surface and can easily be washed away. In the lower salt marsh zones, *Puccinellia*, which is tolerant of waterlogging (Brereton 1971; Gray & Scott 1977a & b; van Diggelen 1987), is found only within *Spartina* stands (Kamps 1962).

— radial oxygen loss from *Spartina* rhizomes (Lambers 1979; Rozema, Luppes & Broekman 1985b), and thus protection against harmful effects of anaerobiosis and low redox potentials, enabling deeper root penetration.

— structural improvement of the upper soil layer by *Spartina* litter, of which shallow-rooted species, such as *Puccinellia*, can take advantage.

— increased surface elevation by accretion of silt around *Spartina* shoots (Ranwell 1972), and thus a lower inundation frequency and improved drainage. On the wadden-type salt marsh at Schiermonnikoog, the centre of a *Spartina* tussock can be up to 20 cm higher than the periphery.

The establishment of other species in a *Spartina* stand is hampered by interspecific competition, largely acting through light reduction. Figure 7 shows that the density of *Salicornia* is lowered with increasing shoot density of *Spartina*, except for a gully where sparse *Spartina* protects *Salicornia* against being washed away (Scholten *et al.* 1987). The centre of a *Spartina* tussock with low shoot density can be reinvaded by *Spartina* through vegetative spread from the peripheral zone (Caldwell 1957), but Chater and Jones (1957) noted an invasion of other species (especially *Puccinellia*) in these less vigorous central parts of the tussocks.

Species can invade or compete successfully with *Spartina* by earlier annual shoot development. *Spartina* does not start growth until April, reaching its maximum growth rate in July (Groenendijk 1984; Long *et al., p35*). This characteristic may be related to the relative cold-sensitivity of *Spartina* (Kamps 1962; Beeftink 1965) or to a high light requirement due to its C_4 photosynthesis pathway (Long & Incoll 1979). *Spartina* rhizomes do not seem to contain enough food reserves for rapid emergence in spring (Long *et al., p36*), such as in *Scirpus maritimus* or *Phragmites australis*. At higher salt marsh elevations, the development of *Spartina* is delayed even more (Taylor & Burrows 1968), suggesting that other species can establish more successfully there. For example, although mature plants of *Aster tripolium*, emerging from taproots in March, can maintain themselves in dense *Spartina* swards at lower

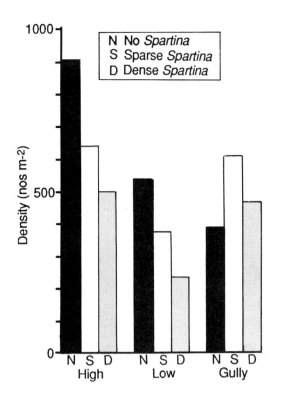

FIGURE 7. *Density of* Salicornia *at sites with no* Spartina, *sparse* Spartina *cover and dense* Spartina *cover at 10 cm below mean high water level (high), at 20 cm below MHW (low) and at 15 cm below MHW within a gully (gully)*

marsh levels, seedlings germinating in April are unable to survive. At higher levels, however, even *Aster* seedlings can survive (H Schat pers. H comm.; Huiskes, van Soelen & Markusse 1985).

In this paper, we have demonstrated the competitive advantage which *Puccinellia* gains from early seasonal growth by pre-empting physical space and shading emergent *Spartina* shoots. The advantage of *Puccinellia* over *Spartina* increases progressively with time, especially on sand. Where both species co-exist, slight differences in abiotic factors can completely reverse the competitive relationships between them. This fact can help to explain the differences between the two Dutch salt marsh areas. The wadden area has a more sandy soil, high salinity, a smaller tidal amplitude, and lower temperatures in spring than the delta area (Dijkema 1984). These characteristics, particularly the soil factors, lead to reduced tussock spread and shoot density of *Spartina* and to the general competitive advantage of *Puccinellia* over *Spartina*, which may explain the occurrence of invaded *Spartina* tussocks, and the gradual replacement of *Spartina* by *Puccinellia*. In the delta area, environmental factors, particularly the clayey soil, lead to the formation of dense, monospecific *Spartina* swards, with a rapid growth of *Spartina* and with *Puccinellia* unable to compete under such conditions. Consequently, the *Spartina* sward persists until degeneration (*cf* 'dieback': Goodman 1960; Goodman & Williams 1961; Goodman *et al.* 1959).

Because it is not replaced by other species, *Spartina* disturbs the natural succession on the lower salt marshes in the delta area (Beeftink 1975, 1977). However, on silty or sandy marshes, such as the wadden-type salt marshes in the wadden area, *Spartina* takes over part of the succession from *Salicornia* to *Puccinellia*. *Spartina* can even facilitate the introduction of *Puccinellia* into the succession. On sandy beach plains, *Spartina* initiates the formation of low dunes.

Grazing or mowing can increase the dominance of *Puccinellia* at the expense of *Spartina* (Ranwell 1961, 1967; Beeftink 1985), and this increase is most strongly demonstrated on well-drained (*viz* sandy) soil, as in the wadden area (Dijkema 1983; and this paper). On clayey soils, however, we have shown that *Puccinellia* fails to invade the shortened *Spartina* stand.

Once more, this study underlines the importance of interspecific plant relations on the zonation and succession of salt marsh vegetation. The influences of environmental factors on plant populations can be fortified or impaired by interspecific interactions with co-existing plant populations. The extension of autecological studies by investigations of plant interactions enables the zonation and succession of salt marsh vegetation to be better understood (eg Goldsmith 1973; Pielou & Routledge 1976; Gray & Scott 1977a; Silander & Antonovics 1982; Beeftink 1985).

6. Acknowledgements

Thanks are due to our colleagues, W Beeftink, P Blaauw, J van Diggelen, T Dueck, W Ernst and H Schat for commenting on previous versions of the manuscript. We also thank P Hoogeveen, T de Nijs and M Stroetenga for their assistance in the glasshouse experiment.

The investigations were supported by the Foundation for Fundamental Biological Research (BION), which is subsidised by the Netherlands Organisation for the Advancement of Pure Research (ZWO; project no. 14–75–023).

7. References

Adams, D.A. 1963. Factors influencing vascular plant zonation in North Carolina salt marshes. *Ecology*, **44**, 445–456.

Allen, E.B. & Forman, R.T. 1976. Plant species removals and old-field community structure and stability. *Ecology*, **57**, 1233–1243.

Beeftink, A. 1985. Interaction between *Limonium vulgare* and *Plantago maritima* in the Plantagini-Limonietum association on the Boschplaat, Terschelling. *Vegetatio*, **61**, 31–44.

Beeftink, W.G. 1965. De zoutvegetatie van ZW–Nederland beschouwd in Europees verband. *Meded. Landbouwhogeschool Wageningen*, **65**, 1–167.

Beeftink, W.G. 1975. The ecological significance of embankment and drainage with respect to the vegetation of the SW Netherlands. *J. Ecol.*, **63**, 423–258.

Beeftink, W.G. 1977. Salt marshes. In: *The coastline*, edited by R.S.K. Barnes, 93–121. London: Wiley.

Beeftink, W.G. 1985. Vegetation study as a generator for population and physiological research on salt marshes. *Vegetatio*, **62**, 469–486.

Brereton, A.J. 1971. The structure of the species populations in the initial stages of salt-marsh succession. *J. Ecol.*, **59**, 321–338.

Caldwell, P.A. 1957. The spatial development of *Spartina* colonies growing without competition. *Ann. Bot.*, **21**, 203–214.

Causton, D.R. & Venus, J.C. 1981. *The biochemistry of plant growth.* London: Edward Arnold.

Chater, E.H. & Jones, H. 1957. Some observations on *Spartina townsendii* in the Dovey estuary. *J. Ecol.*, **45**, 157–167.

Dijkema, K.S. 1983. The salt-marsh vegetation of the mainland coast, estuaries and halligen. In: *Flora and vegetation of the Wadden Sea islands and coastal areas. Report 9, Ecology of the Wadden Sea,* edited by K.S. Dijkema & W.J. Wolff. Rotterdam: Balkema.

Dijkema, K.S. 1984. Western-European salt-marshes. In: *Salt marshes in Europe,* edited by K.S. Dijkema. (Nature and Environment series no. 30.) Strasbourg: Council of Europe.

Fowler, N. 1984. Competition and coexistence in a N. Carolina grassland. II. The effects of the experimental removal of species. *J. Ecol.*, **69**, 843–854.

Goldsmith, F.B. 1973. The vegetation of exposed sea-cliffs at South Stack, Anglesey. II. Experimental studies. *J. Ecol.*, **61**, 819–929.

Goodman, P.J. 1960. Investigations into 'die-back' in *Spartina townsendii*. II. The morphological structure and composition of the Lymington sward. *J. Ecol.*, **48**, 711–724.

Goodman, P.J., Braybrooks, E.M. & Lambert, J.M. 1959. Investigations into 'die-back' in *Spartina townsendii*. I. The present status of *Spartina townsendii* in Britain. *J. Ecol.*, **47**, 651–677.

Goodman, P.J. & Williams, W.T. 1961. Investigations into 'die-back' in *Spartina townsendii*. III. Physiological correlates of 'die-back'. *J. Ecol.*, **49**, 391–398.

Gray, A.J. & Scott, R. 1977a. The ecology of Morecambe Bay. VII. The distribution of *Puccinellia maritima, Festuca rubra* and *Agrostis stolonifera* in the salt marshes. *J. appl. Ecol.*, **14**, 229–241.

Gray, A.J. & Scott, R. 1977b. *Puccinellia maritima.* (Biological flora of the British Isles.) *J. Ecol.*, **65**, 699–716.

Groenendijk, A.M. 1981. *Effekten van verlengde inundatieduur op de groei en de ontwikkeling van een aantal schorreplanten.* (VEGIN-rapport no. 1.) Middelburg: Rijkswaterstaat.

Groenendijk, A.M. 1984. Primary production of four dominant salt-marsh angiosperms in the SW Netherlands. *Vegetatio*, **57**, 143–152.

Hubbard, J.C.E. 1965. *Spartina* marshes in southern England. VI. Patterns of invasion in Poole Harbour. *J. Ecol.*, **53**, 799–813.

Hubbard, J.C.E. 1969. Light in relation to tidal immersion and the growth of *Spartina townsendii. J. Ecol.*, **57**, 795–804.

Huiskes, A.H.L., van Soelen, L. & Markusse, M.M. 1985. Field studies on the variability of populations of *Aster tripolium* in relation to salt-marsh zonation. *Vegetatio*, **61**, 163–169.

Hussey, A. & Long, S.P. 1982. Seasonal changes in weight of above and below ground vegetation and dead plant material in salt marsh at Colne Point, Essex. *J. Ecol.*, **79**, 757–771.

Kamps, L.F. 1962. *Mud distribution and land reclamation in the eastern Wadden shallows.* Den Haag: Rijkswaterstaat.

König, D. 1948. *Spartina townsendii an der Westküste von Schleswig-Holstein. Planta*, **36**, 34–70.

Lambers, H. 1979. *Energy of metabolism in higher plants in different environments.* Thesis, Groningen.

Long, S.P. & Incoll, L.D. 1979. The prediction and measurement of photosynthetic rate of *Spartina townsendii* in the field. *J. appl. Ecol.*, **16**, 879–891.

Morley, J.V. 1972. Tidal immersion of *Spartina* marsh at Bridgwater Bay, Somerset. *J. Ecol.*, **60**, 383–386.

Pielou, E.C. & Routledge, R.D. 1976. Salt marsh vegetation: latitudinal gradients in the zonation patterns. *Oecologia*, **24**, 311–321.

Ranwell, D.S. 1961. *Spartina* salt marshes in southern England. I. The effects of sheep grazing at the upper limits of *Spartina* marsh in Bridgwater Bay. *J. Ecol.*, **49**, 325–340.

Ranwell, D.S. 1967. World resources of *Spartina townsendii* and the economic use of *Spartina* marshland. *J. appl. Ecol.*, **4**, 239–256.

Ranwell, D.S. 1972. *Ecology of salt marshes and sand dunes.* London: Chapman & Hall.

Rozema, J., Bijwaard, P., Prast, G. & Broekman, R. 1985a. Ecophysiological strategies of coastal halophytes from sand dunes and salt marshes. *Vegetatio*, **62**, 499–522.

Rozema, J., Luppes, E. & Broekman, R. 1985b. Differential response of salt-marsh species to variation of iron and manganese. *Vegetatio*, **62**, 293–301.

Scholten, M.C.T., Blaaww, P., Stroedenga, M. & Rozema, J. 1987. The impact of competitive interactions on the growth and distribution of plant species in salt marshes. In: *Vegetation between land and sea,* edited by A.H.L. Huiskes, C.W.P.M. Blom & J. Rozema, 260–279. Dordrecht: Junk.

Silander, J.A. & Antonovics, J. 1982. Analysis of interspecific interactions in a coastal community – a perturbation approach. *Nature, Lond.*, **298**, 557–560.

Sokal, R.R. & Rohlf, F.J. 1981. *Biometry.* 2nd ed. San Francisco: Freeman.

Spitters, C.J.T. 1983. An alternative approach in the analysis of mixed cropping experiments. I. Estimation of competition effects. *Neth. J. agric. Sci.*, **31**, 1–11.

Taylor, M.C. & Burrows, E.M. 1968. Studies on the biology of *Spartina* in the Dee estuary, Cheshire. *J. Ecol.*, **56**, 795–809.

Van Diggelen, J. 1987. *A comparative study on the ecophysiology of salt marsh halophytes.* PhD thesis, Free University of Amsterdam.

Wit, C.T.de 1960. On competition. *Versl. Landb. Onderz. Wageningen*, **66**, 1–82.

CHAPTER 8

Spartina as a biofuel

R Scott, T V Callaghan and G J Lawson

Institute of Terrestrial Ecology, Merlewood Research Station, Grange-over-Sands, Cumbria, LA11 6JU

Summary

In 1980 a production trial was established at Southport to find the optimal harvest time for *Spartina anglica* as a biofuel. Yield fell from 16 dry tonnes ha^{-1} yr^{-1} to 8 t ha^{-1} yr^{-1} after three years in autumn- and winter-harvested plots. Application of fertiliser gave no significant increase in yield, so it was assumed that nutrients were not limiting growth. Biomass became much lower in summer-harvested plots and *Puccinellia maritima* was increasingly dominant. Costs of harvesting and energy conversion of *S. anglica* are likely to be high compared with other biofuels. High ash content will reduce the efficiency of conversion. *S. anglica* sites could still be useful locally as a fuel source because of their high productivity and lack of existing economic value.

1. Introduction

Several workers have examined ways of using *Spartina anglica* since its evolution last century. Ranwell (1967) has reviewed its uses worldwide. Oliver (1925) introduced it to a number of sites with the aim of enhancing the consolidation of mudflats. In the USA, Broome, Woodhouse and Seneca (1975) have planted *S. alterni-*

flora to bind dredged spoil. In the People's Republic of China, the Institute of Rice Grass and Tidal Land Development has based research on ramets originating from Britain (Chung 1983) and large areas of *S. anglica* now exist (see Chung, p72).

The UK Department of Energy (King 1984) has funded research into renewable sources of energy, which included biomass as part of the programme. The Institute of Terrestrial Ecology carried out a preliminary assessment of a range of naturally occurring plant species as energy crops in Great Britain (Callaghan, Scott & Whittaker 1981). Other nations, eg France (Chabbert *et al.* 1985), have invested much larger funds than Britain in research on biofuels from plants such as Jerusalem artichoke and Mediterranean giant reed (*Arundo donax*). In the USA, Pratt, Dubbe & Andrews (1983) have carried out detailed work on wetland plants, notably *Typha latifolia*, as potential energy crops. In Sweden, a research and demonstration project uses reed as a fuel crop (Graneli 1984). Harvesting is in winter on frozen lakes using Seiga low-ground density amphibious vehicles (see Figure 1). However, in the UK, it is unusual for natural vegetation to be used for any other purpose than rough grazing. Reed (*Phragmites*

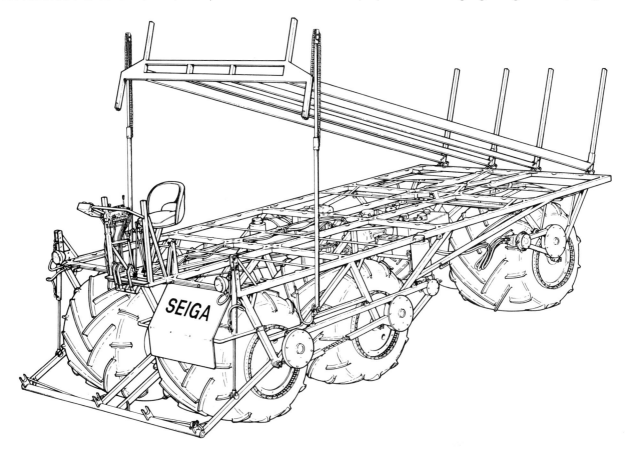

FIGURE 1. *Low-ground density Seiga harvester as used in Sweden for reed cropping on similar terrain to salt marshes*

australis) as roofing thatch, and bracken (*Pteridium aquilinum*) for animal bedding are examples of current minor uses.

Spartina anglica was included in our search for wild plant species which might be usable as biofuel crops. It fulfils the criterion of being vigorous and productive, though, as with other species, precise data on aerial yield were not readily available in the literature. The plant has other features which make it a candidate for use. It is often an unwelcome invader, and cropping offers a means of transforming sites into more acceptable vegetation. Sites are level and would be relatively easy to harvest. However, it has a limited national distribution and it may not be economic to develop processing methods. Biomass conversion could follow a number of routes, for example anaerobic digestion to methane (White & Plaskett 1981) or by pyrolysis to a range of gases, tars and char (Bridgwater 1984). This paper summarises the ecological aspects of cropping *S. anglica* in the UK as a biofuel, and examines the harvesting effects.

2. Site and methods

The field site was 200 m north of the sand-winning plant at Southport, Merseyside (SD 354 206), described elsewhere by Robinson (in Doody 1984) and Marks and

Truscott (1985). Whilst root biomass was measured in earlier work (Callaghan *et al.* 1981), this project sampled only aerial shoots. *S. anglica* was known to be late in its growth, so harvests in September, November and January were used to span the period of maximum biomass. In addition to the three harvests, three fertiliser treatments were given, the equivalent of 0.5, 1 and 2 t ha^{-1} of 20:10:10 Fisons agricultural fertiliser (with a zero control), applied as granules in periods of no tidal inundation during the neap tides in May or June. The experimental design was a split plot with four replicate blocks (Callaghan *et al.* 1985), based on 3 m × 3 m treatment squares with a central 1 m × 1 m sample quadrat. The central 1 m was cut with a sickle to ground level and the sample retained. Material from the buffer zone was removed from the site. A 1 m quadrat with 20 cm grid was used to make frequency counts of the species in January before the final cut. Species cover was estimated visually.

3. Results

The yield and nutrient content of the *S. anglica* from the plots cut in November in the first three years of the trial are presented in Figure 2. There was a progressive annual decline, with no significant treatment effect for nutrient application. The early season cuts are associated with reduced cover of *S. anglica* and colonisation

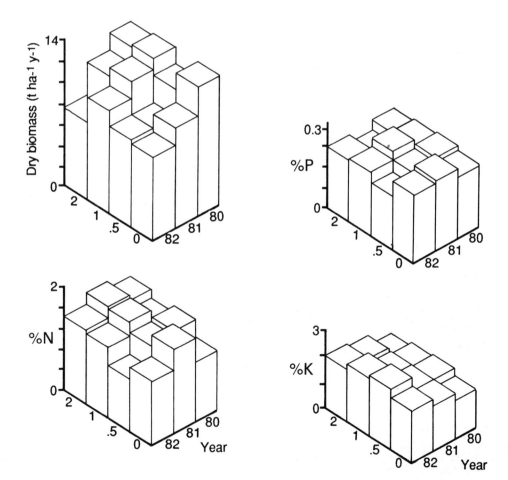

FIGURE 2. Yield and nutrient content of Spartina anglica *in growth trials at Southport, given three fertiliser levels over three annual harvests in November*

49

by *Puccinellia maritima*. Total biomass declined because the colonisers were less productive. January cuts maintained the *S. anglica* cover, and stem density data (Callaghan *et al.* 1985) suggest that the species reacts in a similar way to winter-cropped *Phragmites australis* (Bjorndahl 1985), with increased stem density but no great fall-off in yield. The results obtained confirm a trend toward the virtual elimination from the sward of *S. anglica*, but, even where cover was much reduced, the *S. anglica* remained well distributed in the sward (Figure 3). Repeated summer harvests of *S. anglica* resulted in the replacement of *S. anglica* by *Puccinellia maritima*.

Typically, *S. anglica* thrives in eutrophic, muddy sites where nutrients are unlikely to be the main limit to growth (Morris 1980). The relative effects of nutrients and substratum are unknown, as fine sediment is often associated with eutrophic conditions, so the two are likely to be confounded. A study site at Rampside in Morecambe Bay has a silty substratum and the maximum aerial standing crop was only 6 t ha^{-1} (Callaghan *et al.* 1981). High levels of soil nutrients are important to sustained yield because cropping would remove nutrients from the site.

In this study, we assumed that *S. anglica* grows in sites where nutrients would be quickly replenished. If *S. anglica* could be stimulated by nutrient addition, greater yields might be obtained. The results confirm that nutrients are not limiting growth, and there was no increase from fertiliser application.

Cutting affects shoot growth in other ways than nutrient removal (Ruess, McNaughton & Coughenour 1983), and the changes induced need to be studied. The success of *S. anglica* as a crop will depend on the yield being sustained. Implicit in the proposal to crop *S. anglica* is the lack of current economic value of the salt marsh, and, in strict economic terms, this statement is true, but *S. anglica* occupies areas rich in wildlife and the effects of its removal would be important (Slavin 1983). For birds feeding in intertidal areas, the transformation of stands into short grass sward would be a benefit. Overall, the productivity of the vegetation would be lowered.

Harvest time is critical because salt marsh plant species have different phenologies. Emergence, peak biomass and flowering do not coincide. Some species, eg *Armeria maritima* and *Puccinellia maritima*, flower in May and June, while *S. anglica* is one of the last to flower and in some years still has anthers in late October. In 1979 at Rampside (Callaghan *et al.* 1981), peak yield was in late November, though the year may have been abnormal. Several factors could be involved in late growth. The combination of neap tides and dry weather in summer can severely retard growth. From our observations, there seems to be a lack of control over flowering in *S. anglica* and the production of both spikes and anthers can be erratic. Seed set is unreliable

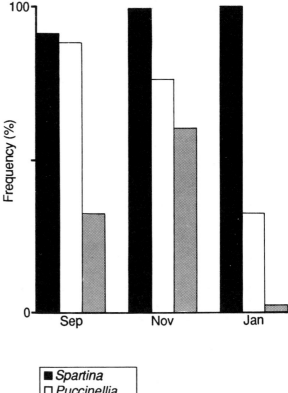

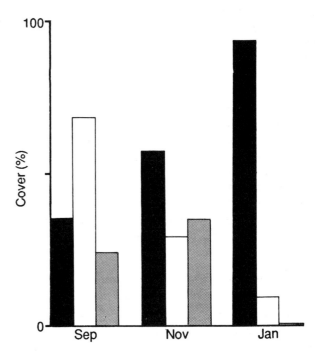

FIGURE 3. *Percentage frequency and estimated cover of* Spartina anglica, Puccinellia maritima *and bare ground in plots cut in September, November and January*

and viability low, with variation between zones on the same marsh. Initiation of flowering greatly alters the composition of the stand in relation to the number of flowering shoots and affects the density of shoots surviving the season.

4. Prospects for use as a fuel

A resource of energy exists in the form of *S. anglica* stands around the British coast, amounting to 120 000 dry t yr^{-1}, using the figure of 12 000 ha of Doody (1984) and a mid-range yield of 10 t ha^{-1}. Measured yields often equal the higher values from intensive arable crops. The biomass produced at present enriches coastal ecosystems. However, the land lacks positive economic value, and control has been necessary in many cases because of the invasion of amenity beaches. While harvesting will not return the saltings to the bare substratum that existed before, the visual impact of short turf comprising other salt marsh grasses is much more acceptable than *S. anglica*. The sustenance of yield is not, therefore, important if *S. anglica* is regarded as a nuisance, and its transformation to short turf would be regarded as an improvement. Summer and early autumn croppings will encourage this change and salt marsh dominated by *Puccinellia maritima* will result, with a consequent loss of production. To sustain the yield of *S. anglica*, harvesting should be from November onwards.

Cropping should not be left too long in the winter because of the build-up of silt on leaves, which will reduce the efficiency of converting the crop to fuel. The risk of flattening by storms and ice crusts increases, making harvesting difficult and further reducing crop quality. The ash content of the aerial biomass is already high because of silica cytoliths (Wynn-Parry & Smithson 1964), but external contamination adds to this internal source the sediment trapped from the autumn tides.

Low-ground pressure vehicles will have to be used for the harvest (see Figure 1). These machines are of the type used for reed harvesting in Sweden and can work in water. Fuel would be produced by a wet feedstock conversion method, either in an anaerobic digester (White & Plaskett 1981) or possibly by a gasification process (Bridgwater 1984). The possibility of combining *S. anglica* biomass with other feedstocks, and also the effluent from sewage treatment, should be considered.

5. Acknowledgements

We thank the UK Department of Energy for funding this work, though the recommendations contained in the paper are ours, and may not reflect official policy. H A Ridsdale, A M Mainwaring, A Millar and several others helped with field work and processed the samples. Thanks are due to the Metropolitan Borough of Sefton for permission to use the site, and to A J Truscott for his co-operation.

6. References

Bjorndahl, G. 1985. Influence of winter harvest on stand structure and biomass production of the common reed, *Phragmites australis* (Cav.) Trin. in Lake Takern, Southern Sweden. *Biomass*, **7**, 303–319.

Bridgwater, A.V. 1984. *Thermochemical processing of biomass.* London: Butterworths.

Broome, S.W., Woodhouse, W.W. & Seneca, E.D. 1975. The relationship of mineral nutrition to the growth of *Spartina alterniflora* in North Carolina. II. The effects of N, P and Fe fertilizers. *Proc. Soil Sci. Soc. Am.*, **39**, 301–307.

Callaghan, T.V., Scott, R. & Whittaker, H.A. 1981. *An experimental assessment of native and naturalised species of plants as renewable sources of energy in Great Britain.* (Natural Environment Research Council contract report to the Department of Energy.) Grange-over-Sands: Institute of Terrestrial Ecology.

Callaghan, T.V., Lawson, G.J., Mainwaring, A.M. & Scott, R. 1985. The effect of nutrient application on plant and soil nutrient content in relation to biomass harvesting. In: *Energy from biomass, 3rd EC Conference*, edited by W. Palz, J. Coombs & D.O. Hall, 412–416. London: Elsevier Applied Science.

Chabbert, N., Giraud, J.P., Arnoux, M. & Galzy, P. 1985. The advantageous use of an early Jerusalem artichoke cultivar for the production of ethanol. *Biomass*, **8**, 233–240.

Chung, C. H. 1983. Geographical distribution of *Spartina anglica* C.E. Hubbard in China. *Bull. mar. Sci.*, **33**, 753–758.

Doody, P. 1984. Spartina anglica *in Great Britain.* (Focus on nature convervation no. 5.) Attingham: Nature Conservancy Council.

Graneli, W. 1984. Reed *Phragmites australis* (Cav.) Trin. ex Steudel as an energy source in Sweden. *Biomass*, **4**, 183–208.

King, C.H. 1984. *An outline of the Department of Energy's biofuels programme.* Harwell: Energy Technology Support Unit.

Marks, T.C. & Truscott, A.J. 1985. Variation in seed production and germination of *Spartina anglica* within a zoned saltmarsh. *J. Ecol.*, **73**, 695–705.

Morris, J.T. 1980. The nitrogen uptake kinetics of *Spartina alterniflora* in culture. *Ecology*, **61**, 1114–1121.

Oliver, F.W. 1925. *Spartina townsendii*: its mode of establishment, economic uses and taxonomic status. *J. Ecol.*, **13**, 74–91.

Pratt, D.L., Dubbe, D.R. & Andrews, N.J. 1983. The development of wetland energy crops in Minnesota, USA. In: *Energy from biomass, 2nd EC Conference*, edited by W. Palz, J. Coombs & D.O. Hall, 386–391. London: Elsevier Applied Science.

Ranwell, D.S. 1967. World resources of *Spartina townsendii* (*sensu lato*) and economic use of *Spartina* marshland. *J. appl. Ecol.*, **4**, 239–255.

Ruess, R.W., McNaughton, S.J. & Coughenour, M.B. 1983. The effects of clipping, nitrogen source and nitrogen uptake of an east African sedge. *Oecologia*, **59**, 253–261.

Slavin, P. 1983. Avian utilisation of a tidally restored salt hay farm. *Biol. Conserv.*, **26**, 271–285.

White, L.P. & Plaskett, L.G. 1981. *Biomass as fuel.* London: Academic Press.

Wynn-Parry, D. & Smithson, F. 1964. Types of opaline silica depositions in the leaves of British grasses. *Ann. Bot. (N.S.)*, **28**, 173–184.

CHAPTER 9

Spartina anglica and oil: spill and effluent effects, clean-up and rehabilitation

J M Baker[1], J H Oldham[2], C M Wilson[3], B Dicks[4]. D I Little[5] and D Levell[5]

[1] *Field Studies Council, Preston Montford, Shrewsbury (present address: Clock Cottage, Ruyton-XI-Towns, Shrewsbury, SY4 1LA)*
[2] *The Leonard Wills Field Centre, Williton, Somerset (present address: Flatford Mill Field Centre, Colchester, Essex)*
[3] *The Leonard Wills Field Centre, Williton, Somerset (present address: Danesfield School, Williton, Somerset)*
[4] *Oil Pollution Research Unit, Orielton Field Centre, Pembroke, Dyfed (present address: International Tanker Owners' Pollution Federation Ltd, Staple Hall, Stonehouse Court, 87–90 Houndsditch, London, EC3A 7AX)*
[5] *Oil Pollution Research Unit, Orielton Field Centre, Pembroke, Dyfed (present address: OPRU, Field Studies Council Research Centre, Fort Popton, Angle, Pembroke, Dyfed, SA71 5AD)*

Summary and conclusions

Spartina anglica survives most single oil spillages by producing new growth from protected underground buds, but does not tolerate chronic pollution (several successive spillages or continuous oily discharges). Light oils penetrate plants and disrupt membrane structures; heavy oils tend to smother plants and may interfere with the normal oxygen diffusion process down the shoots into the roots.

Spartina is capable of recolonising formerly oil-damaged areas (even if the sediments are not completely free of oil residues). Dispersant treatments are not effective in removing oil from *Spartina*, though diluted dispersant alone does not appear to damage the plants. Cutting is a possible clean-up treatment, but it may increase damage in waterlogged areas (perhaps through flooding of oxygen diffusion pathways in the remaining parts of the plants). *Spartina* is capable of producing new growth after burning, but this clean-up technique is difficult to carry out (and would be particularly damaging to many other marsh species). With the oil solidification clean-up technique, there are considerable problems in mixing the solidifying agents into the oil *in situ*. Stripping of oily *Spartina* plus surface sediments, followed by seeding and transplanting, is a drastic and relatively expensive clean-up technique. It has been used successfully on a heavily oiled *Spartina alterniflora* marsh in the USA.

Oil is not likely to penetrate far into waterlogged mud, but, in relatively well-drained sediments, it may penetrate and be retained (particularly in the top 10 cm) for many months or years.

Spartina dieback is widespread in the oil port of Milford Haven. The dieback characteristics are similar to those previously reported from the Southampton Water/Lymington areas in the south of England. It is suggested that the primary cause of dieback is fine sediments accumulated by *Spartina* over 30 years. However, petrogenic hydrocarbons (and possibly other pollutants) tend to accumulate in fine sediments and cannot be entirely ruled out as a factor contributing to dieback.

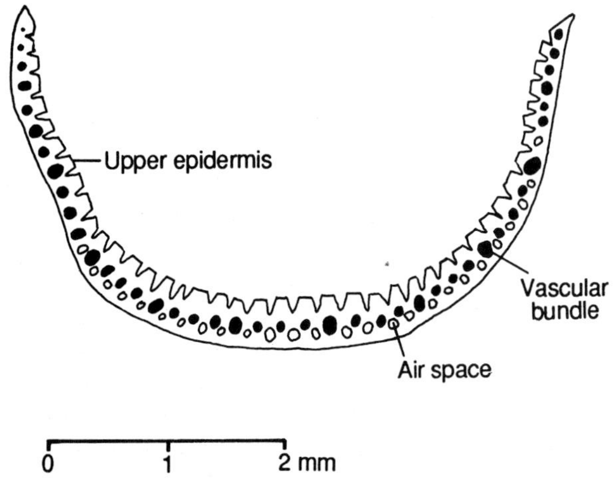

1. Oil industry activities which may affect *Spartina*

In many estuaries, *Spartina anglica* marshes co-exist with oil industry installations, and *Spartina* may be subjected to a variety of disturbances resulting from oil industry activities. The three main categories of these are oil spills, spill clean-up activities, and operational discharges. *Spartina* marshes tend to act as oil traps because they occur in sheltered, low-energy environments, because they are in the strandline zone, and because the vegetation offers a large surface area for oil absorption, its leaves being present in high densities, and each individual leaf having a corrugated upper surface (Figure 1).

1.1 *Oil spills*

These incidents may include spills of various sizes following tanker accidents; numerous small spills from all types of shipping; blow-outs; and spills from damaged pipelines. The following categories of oil spills (Dudley 1976) are particularly likely to occur in ports or at oil terminals:

- fairly frequent spillages involving a few gallons, caused by minor overflows of cargo tanks, tank-cleaning operations, malfunctions of sea valves, carelessness during the connecting and disconnecting of hoses, and sometimes by breaking the rules, such as pumping bilges. They may occur anywhere within a port and are not restricted to operations at terminals, or specifically to oil tankers.

FIGURE 1. *Cross-section of* Spartina anglica *leaf, showing high surface area of upper epidermis and air spaces*

- infrequent spillages involving up to 5 tons of oil, often resulting from damage or mechanical failure, and most likely to occur during loading or discharging operations in the vicinity of terminals.

Serious and catastrophic spillages from tankers following collision, grounding or other damage are rare compared with the above categories, and may occur anywhere along tanker routes. Well blow-outs are a rare occurrence, but can produce oil spills of considerable size over a period of time.

1.2 Clean-up

If oil enters a marsh, a number of possible clean-up options may be considered. These options are listed below and have been investigated experimentally, as summarised in section 3. Some are more useful than others but it should be stressed at the outset that misdirected activity can cause more damage than the oil itself.

i. Natural clean-up (the 'do nothing' approach). Some oil may be removed by tidal action and some will be broken down by naturally occurring oil-degrading bacteria, which multiply rapidly under suitable conditions (ie adequate quantities of substrate, nutrients and oxygen). Oil absorbed on *Spartina* plants is likely to be exported from the marsh when the stems and leaves die in winter and break up into detritus. However, under some circumstances, free oil is likely to penetrate sediments where it may persist for many months or years (see section 3.11).

ii. Cutting. Where lightly oiled marshes have to be treated (eg for amenity reasons or because birds are threatened), the cutting and removal of oily stems and leaves (not the wholesale removal of the marsh surface) may be an acceptable treatment, provided that heavy trampling damage can be avoided.

iii. Burning. It may be possible to burn oily standing vegetation without damaging the underground root and rhizome systems.

iv. Stripping. This method is only likely to be justifiable in cases of thick smotherings by potentially long-lived deposits which would kill existing vegetation and prevent recolonisation. Heavy earth-moving equipment is necessary to remove the marsh surface, and there may be subsequent problems with erosion of the subsurface sediments. Thus, stripping should only be considered with replanting.

v. Dispersants. These work by breaking up oil into very small droplets which become suspended and diluted in the water column. Tidal and wave action are important for effective mixing and dilution of the oil and dispersant, so shore application is best done just before the incoming tide.

vi. Gelling. This is a recently developed technique whereby oil is 'solidified' by being mixed with a polymer and cross-linking agent (Meldrum, Fisher & Plomer 1981), which is intended to facilitate its physical removal.

Further information on clean-up methods can be found in Wardley-Smith (1983).

1.3 Operational discharges

Apart from spills and spill clean-up, marshes may also be affected by operational discharges, such as formation water or refinery effluents. These discharges are likely to contain low concentrations of dissolved hydrocarbons, small droplets of oil, and some particulate material with adsorbed oil. Detailed information on refinery effluents can be found in CONCAWE (1979).

2. Mechanisms of oil damage

2.1 Toxicity

A variety of crude oils and oil products has been studied, and it is evident that both crude oils and products differ widely in their toxicity. In general, it appears that severe toxic effects are associated with low-boiling compounds and aromatics. With plants (which have been studied with herbicidal oils in mind), there is experimental evidence that toxicity increases along the series alkanes (paraffins) – cycloalkanes (naphthenes) – alkenes (olefins) – aromatics. Within each series of hydrocarbons, the smaller molecules are more toxic than the larger. The literature is reviewed by Baker (1970). Toxic effects result from penetration of plant cells, the plasma membrane being a critical structure. Van Overbeek and Blondeau (1954) suggested how hydrocarbons dissolve in the plasma membrane and open it up by displacing fatty molecules. Permeability is thereby increased, and cell sap leaks into the intercellular spaces.

2.2 Smothering

Weathered crude oils or heavy fuel oils are unlikely to produce toxic effects of the type noted above, but may damage plants by blocking their stomata (thus interfering with gas exchange) and absorbing light wavelengths essential for photosynthesis.

Spartina has an oxygen diffusion pathway from the leaves (Figure 1) to the roots (Armstrong 1967). This pathway is probably important for maintaining an oxidised layer round the roots, and thus for preventing damage from toxic reduced ions. There is experimental evidence (Baker 1971a, b) that oil on the leaves can reduce the oxygen diffusion out of the roots; thus, oiling of the aerial parts of the plant may indirectly affect the health of the underground system.

3. Summaries of field experiments on spill and clean-up effects

This section summarises experiments carried out by the Field Studies Council (Oil Pollution Research Unit) in England and Wales. Little other quantitative information is available concerning spill and clean-up effects on *Spartina anglica*. A stripping experiment (section 3.10) carried out on *Spartina alterniflora* in the USA has been included, as we are not aware of a similar experiment with *Spartina anglica*. It is of relevance as stripping may conceivably be considered as a clean-up option for severely oiled British marshes.

3.1 *General experimental design*

Experimental sites, as homogeneous as possible, were chosen in areas of *Spartina anglica* at sites in south Wales or north Somerset (Figure 2). At each site, treatments were applied to marked plots with a randomised block experimental design. In addition to the treated plots, experiments also contained controls. Oil was applied to plots just after the ebbing tide had left them exposed, simulating as closely as possible the stranding of a slick. Dispersant was usually prediluted with sea or estuary water from near the experimental sites – the obvious source of water in real clean-up operations. Dilution rates were those recommended by the dispersant manufacturers, as was the procedure for spraying plots as the tide was rising (to ensure dilution of dispersed oil with a minumum of delay). Quantitative botanical data were collected before experimental treatments and at intervals afterwards. More specific information is given in the following descriptions of individual experiments.

3.2 *Single applications of Kuwait crude oil at different times of year*

Details of this experiment have been published (Baker 1971a, b).

Site: Bentlass salt marsh, Milford Haven, Dyfed.

Experimental plots and treatments: single (unreplicated) 2 m × 2 m plots received the following treatments applied by hand-pumped knapsack sprayer:

i.   2 litres of Kuwait crude oil, May 1968;

ii. 2 litres of Kuwait crude oil, August 1968;

iii. 2 litres of Kuwait crude oil, November 1968;

iv. 2 litres of Kuwait crude oil, February 1969.

Five plots were established, including a control.

Monitoring methods: live *Spartina* cover was measured using point quadrats – a frame of ten pins distributed randomly ten times within each plot.

Results: most of the oil was quickly absorbed by the *Spartina* shoots and was not observed to wash off during subsequent tidal immersions. The cover data (Figure 3) show the normal winter decline, decline caused by oiling, and recovery at different times of year.

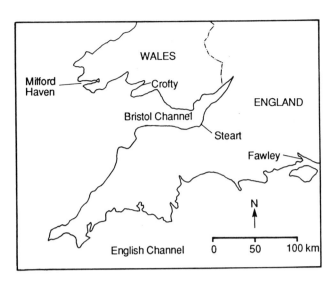

FIGURE 2. South-west Britain, showing locations of sites mentioned in the text. For sites within Milford Haven, see Figure 7

There was little recovery of *Spartina* oiled in August or November until the following growing season; thus, marshes oiled in summer or autumn may appear to be in bad condition for many months, even though recovery is eventually possible.

3.3 *Successive applications of Kuwait crude oil*

Details of this experiment have been published (Baker 1971a, b).

Site: Crofty salt marsh, near Llanridian, West Glamorgan.

Experimental plots and treatments: duplicate 2 m × 5 m plots received the following treatments applied by hand-pumped knapsack sprayer:

i.   4.5 litres of Kuwait crude oil twice, with an interval of one month, for a total of 9 litres;

ii. 4.5 litres of Kuwait crude oil four times at monthly intervals, for a total of 18 litres;

iii. 4.5 litres of Kuwait crude oil eight times at monthly intervals, for a total of 36 litres;

iv. 4.5 litres of Kuwait crude oil 12 times at monthly intervals, for a total of 54 litres.

Treatments were started for one block during June 1968 and for the second block during July 1969. Ten plots were established, including controls.

Monitoring methods: live *Spartina* shoots were counted within ten random 25 cm quadrats per plot.

Results: the density data (Figure 4) show that recovery was good from up to four oilings. With eight, and especially with 12, oilings, recovery was slow, depending more on recolonisation from outside the oiled plots than on the growth of surviving plants or rhizomes within the plots.

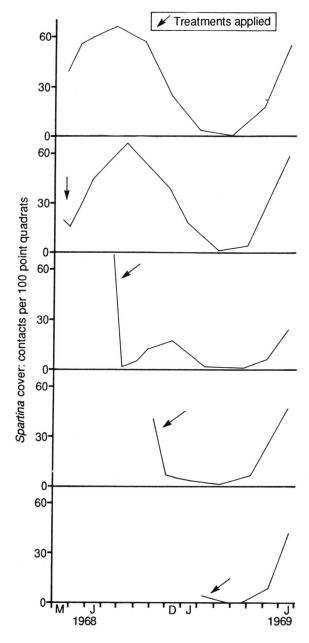

FIGURE 3. *Recovery of* Spartina anglica *from Kuwait crude oil applied during May, August, November and February. Top graph = control*

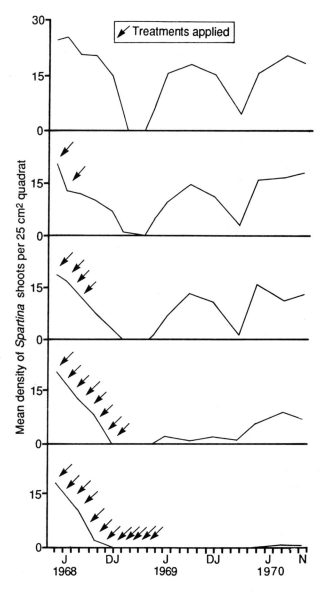

FIGURE 4. *Effects of successive monthly applications of Kuwait crude oil on* Spartina anglica. *Top graph = control*

3.4 *Forties crude oil and BP 1100 WD dispersant (1)*

Details of this experiment have been published (Baker *et al.* 1980; Baker *et al.* 1984).

Site: Steart salt marsh, Bridgwater Bay, Somerset.

Experimental plots and treatments: single (unrepli-cated) 5 m × 3 m plots received the following treatments applied by hand-pumped sprayer during July 1978:

i.   10 litres of Forties crude oil;

ii. 4 litres of diluted BP 1100 WD dispersant (1:9);

iii. 10 litres of Forties crude oil followed by 4 litres of diluted BP 1100 WD.

Four plots were established, including a control.

Monitoring methods: to avoid damage to the vege-tation from trampling, pairs of rails about 60 cm high were set up along the sides of each plot, and a ladder was laid across them when required. Densities of *Spartina* shoots were recorded with ten random 20 cm × 20 cm quadrats per plot. To minimise edge effects, quadrats were not located within a 25 cm border area inside each plot boundary. *Spartina* shoot heights and the density of flowering spikes were also recorded.

Results: some of the oil was quickly absorbed by the *Spartina* shoots and was not observed to wash off during subsequent tidal immersions. In this respect, there was no obvious visual difference between untreated and dispersant-treated oil. Some of the oil (unquantified) is assumed to have evaporated.

Spartina data for 1978 and 1979 have been published (Baker *et al.* 1980). These and subsequent unpublished data show that, during the first three months after treatments, there was a gradual decline in *Spartina* density in the oiled plot, but this decline was not statistically significant when compared with the control. From four to 26 months after treatment, there was a significant reduction in density in the oiled plot, after which this plot did not differ significantly from the control. In the oil followed by dispersant plot, there was a significant reduction in density, as compared with the control, from four to 15 months after treatment. The oiled plot showed significant reduction in density, compared with the oil followed by dispersant plot, from 19 to 25 months after treatment. Dispersant alone appeared to have no effect on *Spartina* density. None of the treatments appeared to affect *Spartina* height. Reductions in numbers of flowering spikes generally parallelled reductions in shoot density. The statistical test used in each case was the Mann–Whitney U test and a reduction was considered significant when P = 0.05 or less.

3.5 *Forties crude oil and BP 1100 WD dispersant (2)*

An account of this experiment has been published (Baker *et al.* 1984).

Site: Steart salt marsh, Bridgwater Bay, Somerset.

Experimental plots and treatments: duplicate 4.5 m × 2.5 m plots received the following treatments during July and August 1979:

i. 7 litres of Forties crude oil twice, for a total of 14 litres;

ii. 5 litres of diluted BP 1100 WD dispersant (1:9), twice, for a total of 10 litres;

iii. 7 litres of Forties crude oil followed by 5 litres of diluted BP 1100 WD, twice, for a total of 14 litres of oil and 10 litres of dispersant.

The two treatments were applied to each plot with a one-month interval between them. There were eight plots, including controls.

Monitoring methods: methods were the same as for the previous experiment, with the following addition: sediment samples were taken at 5 cm intervals (from 0 to 25 cm) from the side of a sampling pit, both before treatment and in May 1981, for hydrocarbon analysis by gas-liquid chromatography. This addition was to find the extent of hydrocarbon penetration and retention in the sediments. Analysis followed published approaches (Baker *et al.* 1984).

Results: dispersant application did not appear to be effective in promoting the removal of oil from vegetation. Following the first tidal immersion, there was no obvious visual difference between plots which had received oil only and plots which received oil followed by dispersant spray. Figure 5 illustrates the effects on *Spartina*. Recovery from the oil treatment did not reach control levels, even after 26 months. There was, however, a steady increase in density. In contrast to

the previous experiment, the oil followed by dispersant plots still showed a significant reduction (Mann–Whitney U test, P = 0.05 or less) in density of *Spartina* after 26 months. There was no significant difference between the oil and oil followed by dispersant treatments. With the dispersant only treatments, a significant reduction in *Spartina* density was recorded on some post-treatment sampling dates, but not consistently. *Spartina* heights were not significantly affected by any of the treatments. Reductions in numbers of flowering spikes parallelled reductions in shoot density. There was no detectable retention of the experimental oil in the sediment samples of May 1981.

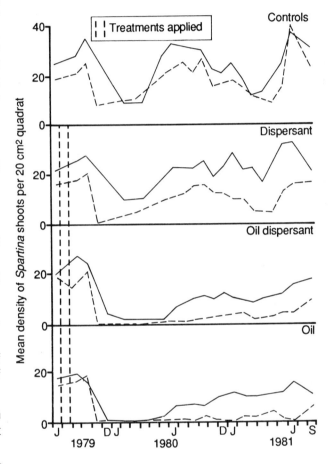

FIGURE 5. *Effects of Forties crude oil and BP 1100 WD dispersant on* Spartina anglica

3.6 *Forties crude oil, residue, mousse and Corexit 7664 dispersant*

An account of this experiment has been published (Baker *et al.* 1984).

Site: Steart salt marsh, Bridgwater Bay, Somerset.

Experimental plots and treatments: duplicate 2 m × 2 m plots received the following treatments at the beginning of August 1981:

i. 10 litres of 'lightly weathered' Forties crude (topped until no dodecane remained) applied by hand sprayer;

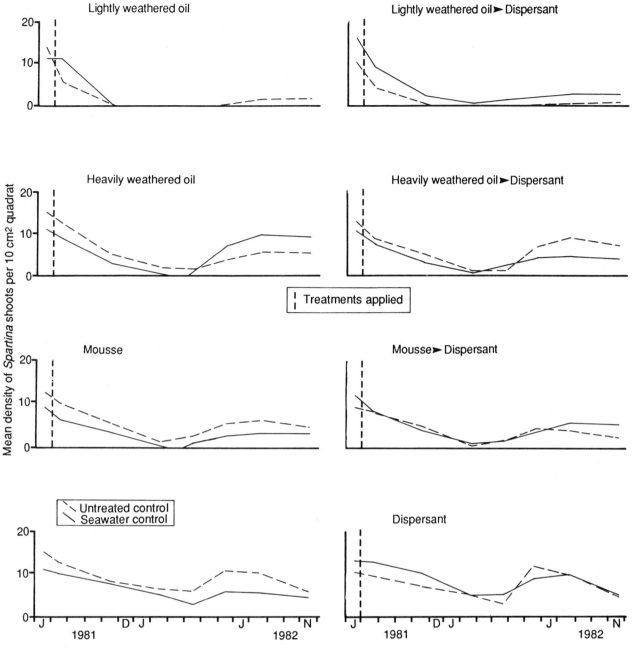

FIGURE 6. *Effects of three different oils and Corexit 7664 dispersant on* Spartina anglica

ii. 16 litres of 'heavily weathered' Flotta crude (ex-refinery residue, n−C=20+) applied by trowel;

iii. 24 litres of mousse (from the *Christos Bitas*, average water content 28% v/v, n−C=13+) applied by trowel;

iv. 120 litres of 2% Corexit 7664 applied by pump delivering at 345 kPa (50 psi);

v-vii. the same as (i) to (iii) above, but followed by 120 litres of 2% Corexit 7664 applied by pump delivering at 345 kPa (50 psi).

Sixteen plots were therefore established, including two control plots.

Monitoring methods: again, a rail and ladder system was used for sampling to overcome trampling damage problems. Ten permanent, randomly located 10 cm

quadrats in a central area of 1 m² in each plot were used for monitoring changes in the density and shoot height of *Spartina*.

Results: visual observations during dispersant spraying and subsequent tidal immersion indicated that the oil that was most effectively removed by the dispersant spray was the lightly weathered Forties crude. Even so, removal was far from complete, and redistribution of washed-off oil by the tide repolluted part of one plot. In the case of 'heavily weathered' Flotta crude, dispersant-treated plots were visually indistinguishable from plots that had not been so treated. Some mousse was removed by the dispersant, but leaves remained patchily contaminated and the plots as a whole still appeared badly oiled after the dispersant treatment. Results (Figure 6) show that the oil treatments significantly reduced the density of live *Spartina* shoots

(Mann–Whitney U test), and this reduction was most severe and prolonged in the slightly weathered Forties crude plots. The dispersant had little or no effect on its own, and did not noticeably alleviate the effects of heavily weathered oil and mousse. However, in one of the plots treated with Forties crude oil followed by dispersant, there was slightly better recovery by late 1982 than was the case with Forties crude oil only. There were no consistent differences between the plots with 'heavily weathered' oil and those with mousse only. Recovery of treated plots started during spring 1982, though it was slight at that time for the Forties crude oil treatments. During the recovery period, up until April 1982, the median value for plant height in the 'heavily weathered' oil plots was about twice that of the control, while the median value for the mousse plots was rather less than twice the control because of the greater height variation.

3.7 Cutting

An account of this experiment has been given by Baker (1971a, b).

Site: Llanstadwell, Milford Haven, Dyfed.

Experimental plots and treatments: light Arabian crude oil accidentally spilt from a refinery on 1 November 1968 affected a small area of *Spartina* marsh. The oily shoots were cut by beach-cleaning contractors and removed for burning. Two treated areas (oiled and cut) and one control area (not oiled or cut) were monitored. Each area was approximately 5 m × 5 m.

Monitoring methods: counts of live shoots were made within ten randomly selected 25 cm × 25 cm quadrats per monitoring area.

Results: in general, new growth occurred over most of the affected area during 1969, but there were a few dead patches, such as Area 1 in Table 1, which persisted. This area is at the lower end of the marsh, which is relatively wet and which may possibly have accumulated oily drainage from elsewhere on the marsh.

Table 1. Llandstadwell: mean number of *Spartina* shoots per 25 cm quadrat, with 95% confidence limits

	2 November 1968 (pre-spill population)	20 August 1969
Area 1 lower marsh. Oiled and cut	26.1 ± 6.3	0.4 ± 0.7
Area 2 mid-marsh. Oiled and cut	23.9 ± 2.7	18.0 ± 2.5
Area 3 upper marsh. Not oiled or cut	27.1 ± 4.7	24.0 ± 3.5

3.8 Burning

An account of this pilot experiment has been given by Baker (1971a, b).

Site: Bentlass salt marsh, Milford Haven, Dyfed.

Experimental plots and treatments: single (unreplicated) 2 m × 5 m plots received the following treatments:

i.   oiled and burnt, April 1969;

ii. oiled, October 1969;

iii. oiled and burnt, October 1969.

Oil application was by means of a hand-pumped knapsack sprayer, and burning was effected using a flame-thrower, because it proved impossible to light the oily *Spartina* with matches (presumably because the volatiles evaporated very quickly). Four plots were established, including a control.

Monitoring methods: counts of live shoots were made within ten randomly selected 25 cm × 25 cm quadrats per plot.

Results: in the 1970 growing season, no significant differences in density of live shoots were found between the various plots.

3.9 Oil solidification

Site: Steart salt marsh, Bridgwater Bay, Somerset.

Experimental plots and treatments: single (unreplicated) 1 m × 1 m plots received the following treatments in April 1982, each carried out using three types of oil (Forties crude, residue and mousse):

i.   oil and solidifying agents pre-mixed, applied to marsh, and removed after solidification;

ii. as (i), but not removed after solidification;

iii. oil applied to marsh, solidifying agents sprayed on and mixed in thoroughly with a rake, and removed after solidification;

iv. as (iii), but not removed after solidification;

v.   oil applied to marsh, solidifying agents sprayed on and left (not mixed in).

Application of pre-mixes simulates what might happen if the oil solidification technique was used in creeks and the results stranded quickly on the vegetation. Oils and pre-mixes were applied using jugs and trowels. On-plot mixing was done using garden rakes. Removal of treated oil, where relevant, was done by hand about 20 minutes after the completion of the treatment, when the oil had become solid. Sixteen plots were established, including a control.

Monitoring methods: a rapid assessment technique was considered to be the most suitable for monitoring vegetation changes, and the Domin cover abundance scale (Mueller-Dombois & Ellenberg 1974) was chosen.

Results: mixing *in situ* was quite effective at incorporating most of the oil with the solidification agents, but the vegetation was damaged in the process. At the time of the experiment, the vegetation was short and without much débris; if treatment was carried out in summer or autumn, when the *Spartina* shoots are much taller, then thorough mixing would be much more difficult to achieve.

The application of solidification agents over oil, without mixing, proved ineffective in taking up the oil, and

58

resulted in free oil being trapped below a mat of solidification agents.

When solidification treatments (all types) were left on experimental plots, there were large declines in *Spartina* cover and only partial recovery during the summer of 1982. Where the solidified oil was removed, there was only a short-term disturbance, particularly in the case of the pre-mix treatments. Removal of the treated oil left small *Spartina* shoots projecting from bare mud, and by July 1982 these plots had similar growths of *Spartina* to the surrounding untreated marsh.

3.10 Stripping

The effects of stripping *Spartina anglica* marshes are not known, but Krebs and Tanner (1981) describe a relevant stripping experiment on a *Spartina alterniflora* marsh in the Potomac River estuary, USA. The marsh was contaminated with heavy fuel oil following an accidental spill. Earth-moving equipment was used to strip oily sediments to just below the rhizome mat, a depth of 7–9 cm. Some plots were back-filled to the original marsh level using material from a local sand pit. Seeding and transplanting of *Spartina alterniflora* was carried out to rehabilitate the plots. In untreated areas of marsh with sediment hydrocarbon concentrations above 10 000 ppm, most of the rhizomes died and little natural regrowth appeared. *Spartina* densities in stripped plots and in the stripped and back-filled plots were similar to the density in the unoiled control by the end of the second growing season.

3.11 Penetration of oil into sediments

If oil penetrates salt marsh sediments, it may persist for many years, with possible long-term effects on plants and animals. Experiments summarised by Baker *et al.* (1984) produced the results given in Table 2. Though most of these experimental sites were not *Spartina*-dominated, the various sediment types covered are all capable of supporting *Spartina* growth, so the results should have predictive value for most types of *Spartina* marsh.

4. *Spartina* in the oil port of Milford Haven

Spartina is believed to have been introduced deliberately into Milford Haven during the 1939–45 war, and was first seen at Sandyhaven and the Gann about 1952 (Dalby 1970). The first record of dieback in the Milford Haven area is that of Dalby (1970), who saw it at the outer edges of a dense sward at Waterloo (western end of the Cosheston River). Dieback at Martinshaven (southern shore of Milford Haven) was subsequently noticed by Baker in 1974, and mapped (Baker 1976). Further dieback was noticed by Baker (unpublished) in Pembroke River in 1980, and it was subsequently decided to carry out a comprehensive investigation of *Spartina* in the whole of the Milford Haven area.

Field survey work was carried out during July and August 1983. Visits were made to all known salt marsh areas where *Spartina* was reported or thought likely to occur, between the mouth of Milford Haven to the west

Table 2. Oil penetration and retention in intertidal sediments

		Steart salt marsh Bridgwater Bay, Somerset	Kilpaison tidal flat, Milford Haven, Dyfed	Steart tidal flat, Bridgwater Bay, Somerset	Sandyhaven tidal flat (1), Milford Haven, Dyfed	Sandyhaven tidal flat (2), Milford Haven, Dyfed
Mean tidal range	Springs	11.1	6.3	11.1	6.3	6.3
	Neaps	6.0	2.7	6.0	2.7	2.7
Sediment facies		Interlaminated sands and muds (bioturbated)	Interbedded sands and muds (anoxic), some *Cardium* sp. shells	Interbedded sands and muds (anoxic), few shells, rippled surface	Current-deposited sand-rippled surface (bioturbated)	Current-deposited sand. Occasional algal mats and silt laminae. Rippled surface
Sediment texture		5% very fine sand laminae in silt/clay matrix	Poorly sorted medium to fine sand with 8–22% silt/clay	Poorly sorted fine to very fine sand with 5–40% silt/clay	Very well-sorted fine to very fine sand with 2% silt/clay	Well-sorted fine to very fine sand with 2–16% silt/clay
Drainage		Moderate, 4–20 cm maximum water table depth	Poor. Surface runoff nearby throughout low tide. 2–5 cm water table depth	Very poor. Only ripple crests drain. 0–2 cm water table depth	Good. 50 cm maximum water table depth	Very good. 60–75 cm maximum water table depth
Oil penetration and retention		No detectable retention of untreated or dispersant-treated oil 21 months after treatments	Retention of untreated and dispersant-treated oil mainly 1–4 cm below surface. More oil retained in dispersant-treated plots (sampling 22–28 months after treatments)	No detectable retention of untreated or dispersant-treated oil ten weeks after treatments	Retention of oil after 12 weeks was found mainly in the 5–10 cm section of oil + dispersant plot	Retention of oil after 12 months with both untreated and dispersant-treated oil. In some cases dispersant treatments increased quantity of oil retained

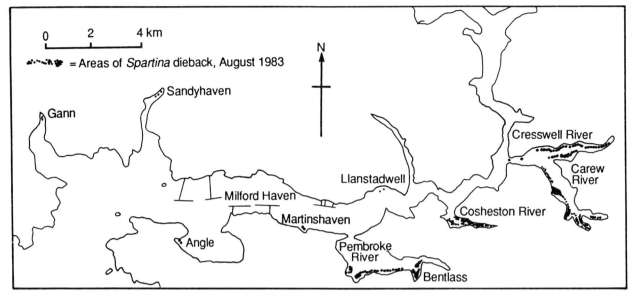

FIGURE 7. *Dieback of* Spartina anglica *in Milford Haven, August 1983*

and the Cresswell/Carew river system to the east. Each area was walked systematically and *Spartina* performance recorded on 1:2500 maps.

Figure 7 is a summary map indicating areas of severe *Spartina* dieback. In most cases, dieback was greatest at the seaward edge of the marshes, where it often formed a distinct zone. There appears to be a relationship between the presence of dieback and soft mud, and in a few cases with creek edges. Oil spillages in the past (Baker 1971a, b) affected some of the marshes visited, namely Sandyhaven, Martinshaven, Llandstadwell and the Pembroke River. Dieback is occurring at all these marshes, but also in the Carew and Cresswell Rivers for which there are no records of spills. Thus, there does not seem to be any obvious relationship between dieback and oil pollution history. However, in another investigation (Oil Pollution Research Unit 1983), a positive correlation was found between the amount of mud in sediments and level of hydrocarbon contamination, and it appears that the soft sediments of the inner Haven act as a sink for at least some of the hydrocarbons entering the Haven. In other words, the adsorptive potential of the finer sediments may determine the ultimate distribution of hydrocarbons at least as much as proximity to oil inputs. Salt marsh sites with no history of oil spills may, therefore, have accumulated some hydrocarbons from the waters of the Haven. Nevertheless, the widespread occurrence of dieback in the Haven, and the similarity with dieback reported from the Southampton Water/Lymington areas, where it was associated with waterlogged, reducing conditions (Goodman & Williams 1961), suggest that the primary cause is fine sediments accumulated by the *Spartina* over 30 years.

5. *Spartina* and refinery effluent

A *Spartina anglica*-dominated salt marsh at Fawley, Southampton Water, which has had refinery effluents discharged through its creek system since 1951, was surveyed in 1969 and 1970 to assess the extent of ecological damage. The salt marsh has been resurveyed every year since 1972 to monitor changes in the distribution of plant species in association with an effluent improvement programme (Figure 8).

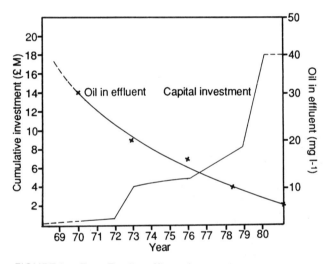

FIGURE 8. *Esso Fawley effluent improvement programme: investment and performance profiles (from Lemlin 1981)*

Full details of the marsh history in association with refinery developments are given by Baker (1971a, b), Dicks (1976), Lemlin (1981), Dicks and Iball (1981), and Dicks and Hartley (1982). They can be summarised as follows.

1950 Aerial photograph taken by the Royal Air Force (RAF) shows the whole marsh area to be covered by healthy *Spartina anglica.*

1951 Outfall no.1 starts operation.

1953 Outfall no. 2 starts operation.

1954 Aerial photograph taken by the RAF shows what can be interpreted as oily vegetation along the edges of the creeks through which the discharges pass.

1962 Photographs of the marsh taken by Dr D S Ranwell show that large areas of *Spartina* have died and decomposed around the two outfalls.

1966 Ordnance Survey map the area and produce sheets nos SU 4404 and SU 4504, showing large areas of bare mud in the effluent discharge area.

1969 A series of transects across the marsh shows extensive areas of bare mud with the remains of *Spartina* stems and roots. The mud level in the denuded area was 15–25 cm lower than in the nearby healthy marsh, indicating differential erosion and/or deposition (Baker 1971a, b).

1970 Resurvey shows little change from 1969. Conclusions reached at this stage (Baker 1971a, b) were that the main damage to the marsh was caused by repeated light oilings from films of oil coming partly from the effluent and partly from spillages.

1972 to the present time, and continuing – regular vegetation mapping surveys show that the formerly denuded marsh has been progressively recolonised, even though some oil residues remain in the sediments. The progress of *Spartina* is illustrated in Figure 9. Recolonisation by the annual *Salicornia* spp. has been even more extensive because of prolific seeding. Transplant experiments indicate that *Spartina* can grow in areas that it has not yet recolonised naturally. Natural *Spartina* recolonisation in this case proceeds by both vegetative growth and by the establishment of some seedlings – a slower process than the spread of *Salicornia*.

6. Acknowledgements

We gratefully acknowledge the financial support of the Department of the Environment (Contract DGR/480/510), the European Commission (Contract ENV-404-UK (N)), the World Wildlife Fund (now the World Wide Fund for Nature), British Petroleum International, and Esso Petroleum Company Ltd (an affiliate of Exxon Corporation).

We should also like to thank·the many people who have assisted with this work, in particular T P Abbiss, M Alexander, S E Howells, S J Rowland and P J C Tibbetts. Staff of the oil companies involved, the Milford Haven Conservancy Board and the Nature Conservancy Council have given helpful advice and co-operation. BP International and Esso Petroleum Co Ltd kindly provided ˙oils, dispersants and solidifying agents, and advised on application.

Figure 9 is published with the kind permission of Esso Petroleum Co Ltd.

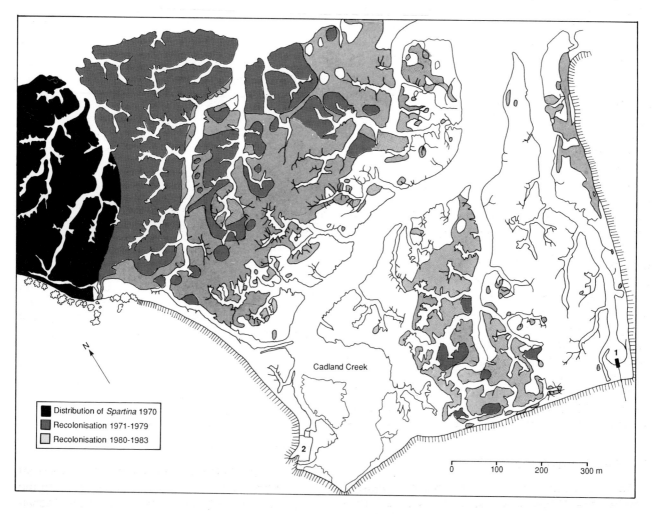

FIGURE 9.   *Recolonisation of Fawley salt marsh by* Spartina anglica. *1 and 2 are refinery effluent discharges*

7. References

Armstrong, W. 1967. The oxidising activity of roots in waterlogged soils. *Physiologia Pl.*, **20,** 920–926.

Baker, J.M. 1970. The effects of oils on plants. *Environ. Pollut.*, **1,** 27–44.

Baker, J.M. 1971a. Studies· on saltmarsh communities. In: *The ecological effects of oil pollution on littoral communities*, edited by E.B. Cowell, 16–101. Barking: Applied Science.

Baker, J.M. 1971b. *The effects of oil pollution and cleaning on the ecology of salt marshes.* PhD thesis, University of Wales.

Baker, J.M. 1976. Ecological changes in Milford Haven during its history as an oil port. In: *Marine ecology and oil pollution*, edited by J.M. Baker, 55–66. Barking: Applied Science.

Baker, J.M., Crothers, J.H., Mullett, J.A.J. & Wilson, C.M. 1980. Ecological effects of dispersed and non-dispersed crude oil: a progress report. In: *Proceedings of the Institute of Petroleum conference on petroleum development and the environment*, 85–100. London: Heyden.

Baker, J.M., Crothers, J.H., Little, D.I., Oldham, J.H. & Wilson, C.M. 1984. Comparison of the fate and ecological effects of dispersed and non-dispersed oil in a variety of intertidal habitats. In: *Oil spill chemical dispersants: research, experience and recommendations*, edited by T.E. Allen, 239–279. Philadelphia: American Society for Testing and Materials.

CONCAWE. 1979. *The environmental impact of refinery effluents.* (Report no. 5/79, pp III–1 – III–77.) Den Haag: CONCAWE.

Dalby, D.H. 1970. The salt marshes of Milford Haven, Pembrokeshire. *Fld Stud.*, **3,** 297–330.

Dicks, B. 1976. The effects of refinery effluents: the case history of a saltmarsh. In: *Marine ecology and oil pollution*, edited by J.M. Baker, 227–245. Barking: Applied Science.

Dicks, B. & Hartley, J.P. 1982. The effects of repeated small oil spillages and chronic discharges. *Phil. Trans. R. Soc.*, **297B,** 285–307.

Dicks, B. & Iball, K. 1981. Ten years of saltmarsh monitoring – the case history of a Southampton Water saltmarsh and a changing refinery effluent discharge. *Proceedings of world oil spill conference (prevention, behaviour, control, cleanup), Atlanta, Georgia, 1981,* 361–374.

Dudley, G. 1976. The incidence and treatment of oil pollution in oil ports. In: *Marine ecology and oil pollution*, edited by J.M. Baker, 27–40. Barking: Applied Science.

Goodman, P.J. & Williams, W.T. 1961. Investigations into 'die-back' in *Spartina townsendii* agg. III. *J. Ecol.*, **49,** 391–398.

Krebs, C.T. & Tanner, C.E. 1981. Restoration of oiled salt marshes through sediment stripping and *Spartina* propagation. *Proceedings of world oil spill conference (prevention, behaviour, control, cleanup), Atlanta, Georgia, 1981,* 375–385.

Lemlin, J.S. 1981. The value of ecological monitoring in the management of petroleum industry discharges: experience in Esso Petroleum Company UK refineries. *Water Sci. Techol.*, **13,** 437–464.

Meldrum, I.G., Fisher, R.G. & Plomer, A.J. 1981. Oil solidifying additives for oil spills. *Proceedings of AMOP conference, Edmonton, 1981,* 325–352.

Mueller-Dombois, D. & Ellenberg, H. 1974. *Aims and methods of vegetation ecology.* London: Wiley.

Oil Pollution Research Unit. 1983. *10th research report.* Pembroke: Field Studies Council.

Van Overbeek, J. & Blondeau, R. 1954. Mode of action of phytotoxic oils. *Weeds*, **3,** 55–65.

Wardley-Smith, H., ed. 1983. *The control of oil pollution.* Revised ed. London: Graham & Trotman.

CHAPTER 10

The response of *Spartina anglica* to heavy metal pollution

J Rozema, M L Otte, R Broekman, G Kamber and H Punte

Ecophysiology Section, Department of Ecology & Ecotoxicology, Free University, PO Box 7161, 1007 MC Amsterdam, Netherlands

Summary

Spartina anglica occurs across a wide range of salt marsh conditions, including a range of sediments polluted with heavy metals. Because it is possible to exclude these metals from the shoot tissue, *Spartina* is not a suitable species for estimating the availability of heavy metals by bioassay or for monitoring their levels. Dicotyledonous species such as *Aster tripolium*, which transfer metals from the roots to the shoots, appear to be more suitable for these purposes.

1. Introduction

The contamination of estuaries with heavy metals can be attributed to various causes, including direct industrial effluents and the heavy metal load of major rivers. This load has been measured in western Europe in the rivers Elbe, Ijssel, Rhine, Meuse and Scheldt, and the accumulation of heavy metals thoroughly investigated (de Groot, Salomons & Allersma 1976; Salomons & Eysink 1981). In the Dutch delta, there has been increased sedimentation of heavy metals adsorbed to suspended material in deep waterways and harbours and in the freshwater basins (Lake Ijssel and Haringvliet) that developed when the mouths of big rivers were closed. Similar contamination of fluvial and marine environments has occurred along densely populated and heavily industrialised coasts in the USA (Simmers *et al.* 1981).

The costs and consequences of the long-term storage and use of contaminated dredged harbour sediment in coastal environments have created a serious economic and ecological problem (Groenewegen & Nijssen 1985). In Dutch coastal areas, the heavy metal content of fluvial and marine sediment may exceed the maximum acceptable levels used for agricultural soils (Interimwet Bodemsanering 1983). Heavy metal pollution is persistent, and metal contamination of coastal sediments presents a diffuse, large-scale problem (in contrast to local mine waste heaps (Ernst 1974)). It is further complicated in rivers and estuaries by increased concentrations of at least ten species of heavy metals in combination with various other kinds of contamination (organic micro-pollution, eutrophication, oil spills) (Ernst & Joosse-van Damme 1983).

The toxic effects of high total concentrations of heavy metals may be ameliorated by environmental conditions which reduce their (bio)availability. For example, their solubility may be kept low (eg heavy metal sulphides formed under anaerobiosis with a low redox potential), or they may be unavailable through adsorption or complexing with organic substances. There are few published estimates of the bioavailability of heavy metals in coastal sediment. Attempts using chemical extraction procedures (water-soluble, exchangeable, reducible and oxidisable fractions) revealed the differential chemical and adsorptive behaviour of the heavy metals of contaminated fluvial and marine mud (Salomons & Förstner 1984), but it is unclear whether these procedures can reliably predict the bioavailability of heavy metals. Field studies (Beeftink *et al.* 1982) have demonstrated very high heavy metal contents in the tissue of salt marsh plants, with significant between-species variation. More recently, the uptake of heavy metals by salt marsh plants under a range of environmental conditions (non-saline *vs* saline, flooded *vs* non-flooded, sediments with a low *vs* high content of organic matter) has been studied (Huiskes & Nieuwenhuize 1985; Rozema *et al.* 1985c). The possible use of heavy metal concentrations in coastal plant tissue as a bioindicator (or biomonitor) of their availability in estuarine water and sediments has also been considered (Simmers *et al.* 1981).

This paper reviews the available data on heavy metal contamination in Dutch salt marshes, and describes experiments in which *Spartina anglica* is cultured in polluted and non-polluted sediment under a range of environmental conditions.

2. The chemical status of heavy metals in estuarine sediment

Most heavy metals in the salt marsh sediment are present as insoluble salts (eg heavy metal sulphides) or adsorbed or complexed to binding sites or inorganic or organic soil particles (Salomons & Förstner 1984; de Rooij *et al.* 1985). By measuring soil characteristics, such as pH, carbonate content, organic matter content, and the redox potential E_7, the chemical status of some heavy metals may be predicted and their bioavailability partly estimated.

In this study, four different methods of extraction were applied to dried salt marsh sediment samples from the Dutch coast (Figure 1, Table 1).

In the water-soluble fraction, ions are measured that are easily available and can be taken up directly by plants. In the extraction procedure, dried sediment was shaken for two hours with extractant solution and some oxidation of water-soluble substances (eg metal sulphides) to soluble substances may have occurred. The water-soluble fraction of heavy metals in salt marsh sediment is the smallest fraction in the sediment. It is negligible for iron (Fe), manganese (Mn), zinc (Zn) and copper (Cu), but somewhat higher for cadmium (Cd) and lead (Pb) (Table 1).

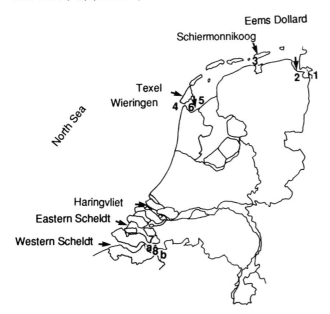

FIGURE 1. *Location of the sampling sites in salt marshes along the Dutch coast of (former) Wadden Islands (Schiermonnikoog, Texel and Wieringen) and the (former) estuaries in south-west Netherlands (Haringvliet, eastern Scheldt, western Scheldt)*

Using 1 M ammonium acetate (pH 7) as an extractant, the ammonium ion replaces heavy metal ions from exchange sites of the inorganic (eg clay) particles or organic compounds in the soil. Similarly, by proton donation of actively growing roots, H^+ ions may be exchanged for cations on the exchange sites of the soil. Therefore, the ammonium acetate exchangeable fraction represents the maximum plant-available fraction of the total soil content of heavy metal ions (Salomons & Förstner 1984). The ammonium acetate (NH_4Ac)-exchangeable fraction of heavy metals including Fe, Mn and other heavy metals is small (Table 1).

The dithionite–citrate–bicarbonate (DCB) method (Jackson 1958; Taylor & Crowder 1983) can be used for the reduction of Fe (III) and Mn (IV) compounds in the soil. Although the citrate in the extractant is meant to complex reduced ions, it may also help to make compounds more soluble. It has been reported (Taylor & Crowder 1983) that 30–40% of the Fe and Mn (hydr)oxides in the soil is DCB-reducible and is found in this fraction. Zn, Cd, Cu and Pb associated with the Fe (III) (hydr)oxides can be found in the DCB-fraction, probably because of being dissolved rather than reduced by the DCB treatment (Table 1).

The total concentration of heavy metals in the estuarine sediment was estimated using a mixed nitric acid/hydrochloric acid extractant (1 M NHO_3/1 M HCl). The variation in concentration at five salt marsh sites along the western scheldt is shown in Figure 2.

Table 1. Heavy metal content of salt marsh sediment (mg kg^{-1} dw) following extraction of four different extractant solutions; average values of four replications. Numbers in brackets indicate location of sampling sites as given in Figure 1.

Sampling site	Fe	Mn	Zn	Cu	Cd	Pb
Eastern Scheldt						
Stroodorpepolder						
H$_2$O	8	0.4	–	–	0.14	3.48
NH$_4$Ac	30.8	2.8	1.9	1.04	0.12	–
Dithionite/citrate	7228	240	14.8	0.48	0.48	4.12
HCl/HNO$_3$	8588	533	76	11.40	1.84	56.00
Bergen op Zoom						
H$_2$O	5.3	5.2	0.6	–	0.13	2.6
NH$_4$Ac	17.6	12	1.2	0.64	0.21	–
Dithionite/citrate	4038	105	8.1	2.8	0.31	3.48
HCl/HNO$_3$	12432	316	39.5	6.2	0.37	10.4
Western Scheldt						
Zandvliet (8b)						
H$_2$O	2.1	1.9	–	–	0.16	3.72
NH$_4$Ac	100	6.4	4.2	0.64	0.30	–
Dithionite/citrate	6244	160	12.0	0.32	0.60	6.0
HCl/HNO$_3$	17680	847	370.0	73.5	8.45	120.2
Bath (8a)						
H$_2$O	3.8	1.9	0.4	–	0.27	3.4
NH$_4$Ac	4.9	7.6	13.6	0.64	1.56	–
Dithionite/citrate	6236	76	26.4	0.6	0.22	5.3
HCl/HNO$_3$	24532	436	241	70.1	3.20	127.6
Wadden area						
Wieringen (5)						
H$_2$O	7.2	8.3	–	–	0.20	3.63
NH$_4$Ac	21.5	62.7	4.6	0.63	0.43	–
Dithionite/citrate	10226	270	12.5	–	0.46	4.95
NCl/HNO$_3$	19367	910	168	22.1	3.3	72.9

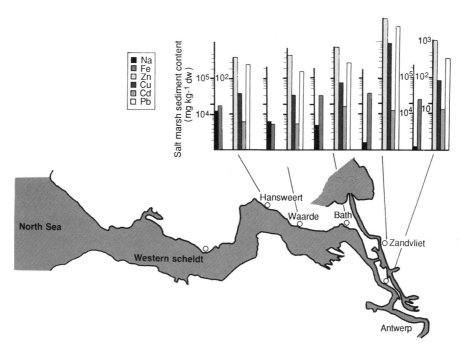

FIGURE 2. The concentration (mg kg^{-1} dw) of Na, Fe, Zn, Cu, Cd and Pb in sediment sampled in western Scheldt estuarine salt marshes along a River Scheldt/North Sea transect

There is dispute about the relative usefulness and ion specificity of different chemical extractants (Salomons & Förstner 1984), and other methods are available (eg Tessier, Campbell & Bisson 1979). Those used here suggest that Cd is the most available of the heavy metals examined, a conclusion also reached by other authors (Salomons & Förstner 1984). However, it is clear that heavy metal uptake studies on plant and animal species will provide important information on the bioavailability and possible biomonitoring function of these organisms.

3. Growth and mineral response of *Spartina anglica* to salinity, flooding and heavy metal pollution

Spartina anglica, which dominates the lower zones of many salt marshes in the Netherlands across a broad range of salinity (Rozema *et al.* 1985b; Scholten & Rozema, p39), is regularly flooded with more or less polluted estuarine water. It may, therefore, be an important species for heavy metal uptake and heavy metal monitoring studies (*cf* Huiskes & Nieuwenhuize 1985).

When grown in natural estuarine sediment, variation in flooding and salinity causes marked changes in biomass production and other plant parameters (eg shoot length) (Rozema *et al.* 1985c). For this reason, when

comparing growth of *Spartina anglica* on polluted (collected from Bath and Zandvliet salt marsh, 8a and 8b, Figure 1) *vs* non (less) polluted salt marsh sediment (collected from Stroodorpe salt marsh, 7, Figure 1), it is difficult to measure differences in growth rate or biomass production that can be ascribed to toxic heavy metal effects. The polluted and non-polluted sediments differ also in other characteristics (eg organic matter content (and therefore redox potential), salinity) (Rozema *et al.* 1985c).

The potential effect of heavy metals on halophyte growth can be assessed more directly from nutrient culture studies (Figure 3) (Rozema, Roosenstein & Broekman 1985a; Rozema & Roosenstein 1985), but it is difficult to translate these results to the field situation. In nutrient solution with 400 mM sodium chloride (NaCl) added, the growth reduction is some 50% compared to growth in solution without NaCl (Figure 3). Under non-saline conditions at 20 μM zinc sulphate (ZnSO$_4$), growth of *Spartina anglica* is 60% of the control. At 5 μM copper sulphate (CuSO$_4$) growth is 63%, and at 50 μM CuSO$_4$ 47% of the control. For Cd, these figures are 75% and 35% at 0.1 μM and 1 μM cadmium sulphate (CdSO$_4$), respectively. Compared with six other salt marsh species (Rozema & Roosenstein 1985), *Spartina anglica* is relatively resistant, particularly compared with *Atriplex littoralis* and *Triglochin maritima* which are severely depressed by the addition of heavy metal salts.

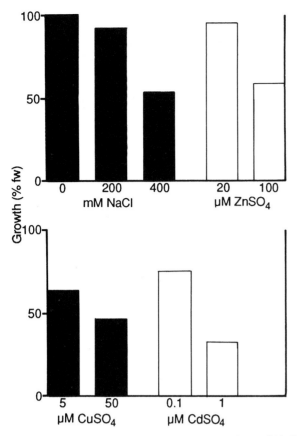

FIGURE 3. The effect of increased concentrations of NaCl, ZnSO₄, CuSO₄ and CdSO₄ in nutrient solution on the growth of Spartina anglica, expressed as a percentage of the fresh weight of root and shoot in the control solution (Hoagland's solution without NaCl and heavy metal sulphates added)

4. Uptake of heavy metals by *Spartina anglica*

Rozema and Roosenstein (1985) report an increase of heavy metals in root and shoot in a variety of salt marsh halophytes, with increasing concentrations in the nutrient culture. Highest concentrations of heavy metals are found in the root tissue, although no distinction was made in our early studies between heavy metals *on* or *in* the root tissue. Secretion of heavy metals of *Spartina anglica* grown in metal-enriched nutrient solution has also been reported elsewhere (Rozema *et al.* 1985). Figure 4 shows the amount of different ions secreted by the salt glands of *Spartina anglica* grown on polluted sediment of the western Scheldt estuary. Although the secretion of Zn and Cu by the salt glands is detectable (Figure 4), its contribution in lowering the heavy metal content of the shoot tissue is relatively small (Rozema *et al.* 1985c).

When grown in polluted salt marsh sediment, *Spartina* plants do not have markedly higher levels of heavy metals in their shoots than when grown in non-polluted sediment. A major fraction of the heavy metals is in the root tissue. Furthermore, the uptake and translocation of heavy metals within the plant are strongly affected by variation in flooding and salinity (Rozema *et al.* 1985a, b, c). The background of variation in growth caused by natural changes in salinity and flooding makes it difficult to detect the effect of heavy metal pollution of the

sediment on the plant's growth response (Rozema *et al.* 1985c). In contrast, other salt marsh species, eg *Aster tripolium* (biennial or short-lived perennial) and *Salicornia brachystachya* (annual), clearly revealed enhanced heavy metal levels in their shoot tissue when grown in heavy metal-polluted salt marsh sediment (Rozema *et al.* 1985c). This finding indicates that heavy metals are excluded from the shoot of *Spartina anglica* more effectively than from *Aster tripolium* and *Salicornia brachystachya*. It also suggests that *Aster* and *Salicornia* are better species for estimating the bio-availability of heavy metals in the salt marsh environment, and for monitoring their levels, than *Spartina anglica*. However, the striking effect of variation in flooding and salinity on heavy metals in the shoot demands that heavy metal uptake pattern can be interpreted only under very closely controlled culture conditions.

As a result of radial oxygen loss or enzymic or bacterial oxidation, iron plaques tend to develop on the roots of plant species in wetland habitats (Smirnoff & Crawford 1983). Using a scanning electron microscope, we have been able to demonstrate the presence of an Fe (III) plaque on the root epidermis of *Spartina anglica*. There were less marked spots of iron detectable in the outer layers of the root cortex. It has been suggested that these iron plaques (identified as alpha- and gamma-Fe OOH-goetthite (Bacha & Hossner 1977)) could be

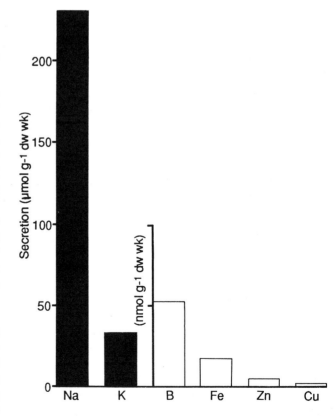

FIGURE 4. Secretion of Na, K (μmol g^{-1} dw wk^{-1}) and B, Fe, Zn and Cu (nmol g^{-1} wk^{-1}) by the salt glands of Spartina anglica grown on polluted western Scheldt (Bath salt marsh 8a, Figure 1). Average values of three replications

involved in the exclusion of heavy metals from the shoots of *Typha latifolia* (Taylor & Crowder 1983). In red roots and rhizomes of *Spartina anglica* plants grown in salt marsh sediment, there were enhanced levels of heavy metals associated with clearly developed iron plaques (extracted by the hot DCB method) compared to ions extracted from white root material (Figure 5).

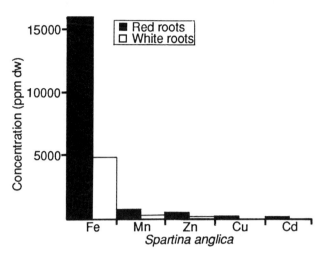

FIGURE 5. Concentrations (mg kg^{-1} dw) of Fe, Mn, Zn, Cu and Cd on the root surface of red and white roots and rhizomes of Spartina anglica *grown in salt marsh sediment from the Bath salt marsh. Average values of four replications*

The monocotyledonous species *Scirpus maritimus*, *Elymus pycnanthus* and *Spartina anglica* show comparatively lower values of Zn, Cu, Cd and Pb in their shoot tissue when grown on contaminated sediment in the glasshouse than dicotyledonous species from the same salt marsh zone. The monocotyledonous species *Trioglochin maritima* also shows relatively low concentrations of the same heavy metals in the shoot tissue. As yet, it is unclear whether the difference in uptake rates of heavy metals between monocotyledonous and dicotyledonous salt marsh species is a general rule.

5. Bioavailability and biomonitoring of heavy metals in salt marshes

As we have mentioned, the complex geochemical conditions in fluvial and marine sediment make it difficult to predict the solubility in water or plant availability of the heavy metal contaminants from the total concentration of heavy metals in the sediment. In addition, the potentially helpful analysis of heavy metal uptake by plants rooting in this sediment is complicated by variations in salinity and flooding conditions (Rozema *et al.* 1985c). Although *Spartina anglica* is possibly a useful species as a heavy metal biomonitor or bioindicator plant, like other coastal monocotyledons it appears to exclude heavy metals from its shoot tissue. Accordingly, there was no significant correlation between the heavy metal content of the salt marsh sediment of the site and the shoot tissue sampled in *Spartina anglica* (Table 2, Figure 6). By contrast, in *Aster tripolium*, a dicotyledonous species, there was a signifi-

Table 2. Concentration of Zn and Cu in salt marsh sediment (sed.) and in aerial parts of *Spartina anglica* (S.a.) and of *Aster tripolium* (A.t.) sampled 21–28 June 1985 on salt marshes along the Dutch coast. Average value of four samples with standard deviation. Location of the sampling sites is indicated in Figure 1

Sampling site		Zn (mg kg^{-1} dw)		Cu (mg kg^{-1} dw)
Eastern Dollard				
(Western Germany)	sed.	31	± 15	3
Dijksterhuizen, Bohrinsel	S.a.	16.7 ±	2.9	2.2 ± 2.9
Western Dollard	sed.	–		38
Karel Coenraat polder	S.a.	53.3 ±	44.5	7.7 ± 1.9
Upper marsh	A.t.	–		6.0 ± 1.6
Karel Coenraat polder creek	A.t.	22.4 ±	1.7	5.1 ± 1.0
Schiermonnikoog	sed.	41	± 18	18
Westerkwelder salt marsh	S.a.	37.4 ±	18.4	6.9 ± 4.2
Texel	sed.	34	± 4	7
Mokbaai salt marsh	S.a.	36.4 ±	5.8	9.3 ± 2.4
Den Oever	sed.	230	± 100	14
Fisher Harbour salt marsh	S.a.	31.0 ±	4.7	6.5 ± 0.9
	A.t.	62.0 ±	5.5	6.5 ± 0.9
Den Helder	sed.	140	± 58	15
Balgzand salt marsh	S.a.	16.9 ±	3.5	9.5 ± 4.5
Eastern Scheldt	sed.	155	± 84	16
Stroodorpe salt marsh	S.a.	13.9 ±	2.6	5.2 ± 1.1
	A.t.	30.1 ±	10.1	13.9 ± 0.9
Western Scheldt	sed.	356		52
Bath salt marsh	S.a.	19.0 ±	4.2	2.0 ± 2.6
	A.t.	56.6 ±	7.9	20.5 ± 9.1
Zandvliet salt marsh	sed.	370		24
(near Antwerp)	S.a.	277	± 11.3	6.1 ± 1.9

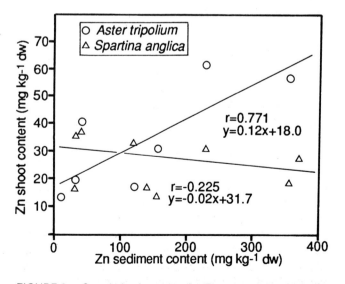

FIGURE 6. *Correlation between the Zn content of the shoot tissue of* Aster tripolium *and* Spartina anglica *at nine salt marshes along the Dutch coast and the Zn content of the sediment sampled at those marshes (see Figure 1)*

cant, positive correlation between the total content of heavy metals in the lower salt marsh sediment samples and the levels found in the aerial parts (Table 2, Figure 6). This result corresponds with glasshouse studies in which dicotyledonous species showed a more marked increase in uptake of heavy metals into the shoot when grown in salt marsh sediment contaminated by heavy metals (Rozema *et al.* 1985c). Clearly, the dicot species such as *Aster tripolium* and *Salicornia* will be more suitable for biomonitoring heavy metals than *Spartina anglica*.

6. References

Bacha, R.E. & Hossner, L.R. 1977. Characteristics of coatings formed on rice roots as affected by iron and manganese additions. *Soil Sci. Soc. Am. J.,* **41,** 931–935.

Beeftink, W.G., Nieuwenhuize, J., Stoeppler, M. & Mohl, C. 1982. Heavy-metal accumulation in salt marshes from the western and eastern Scheldt. *Sci. Total Environ.,* **25,** 199–223.

Ernst, W.H.O. 1974. *Schwermetalvegetation der Erde.* Stuttgart: Fischer.

Ernst, W.H.O. & Joosse-Van Damme, E.N.G. 1983. *Umweltbelastung durch Mineralstoffe.* Jena: Fischer.

Groenewegen, H.J. & Nijssen, J.P.J. 1985. Large-scale disposal of contaminated dredged material from Rotterdam Harbour region. *Proc. int. Conference on Heavy Metals in the Environment, Athens, Greece,* 221–224.

Groot, A.J. de, Salomons, W. & Allersma, E. 1976. Processes affecting heavy metals in estuarine sediments. In: *Estuarine chemistry,* edited by J.D. Burton & P.S. Liss, 131–157. London: Academic Press.

Huiskes, A.H.L. & Nieuwenhuize, J. 1985. Uptake of heavy metals from contaminated soils by salt-marsh plants. *Proc. int. Conference on Heavy Metals in the Environment, Athens, Greece,* 307–309.

Interimwet Bodemsanering. 1983. *Leidraad Milieubeheer (Law and interim soil reconstruction.* The Hague: Ministry of Housing, Physical Planning and Environmental Management.

Jackson, M.L. 1958. *Soil chemical analysis.* Englewood Cliffs: Prentice-Hall.

De Rooij, N.M., Bril, J., Kerkdijk, N.H. & Salomons, W. 1985. Geochemical processes in a large disposal of contaminated sludge. *Proc. int. Conference on Heavy Metals in the Environment, Athens, Greece,* 225–228.

Rozema, J. & Roosenstein, J. 1985. Effects of zinc, copper and cadmium on the growth and mineral composition of some salt-marsh halophytes. *Vegetatio,* **62,** 551–553.

Rozema, J., Roosenstein, J. & Broekman, R. 1985a. Effects of zinc, copper and cadmium on the mineral nutrition and ion secretion of salt secreting halophytes. *Vegetatio,* **62,** 554–556.

Rozema, J., Bijwaard, P., Prast, G. & Broekman, R. 1985b. Ecophysiological adaptations of coastal halophytes from foredunes and salt marshes. *Vegetatio,* **62,** 499–521.

Rozema, J., Otte, M.L., Broekman, R. & Punte, H. 1985c. Accumulation of heavy metals in estuarine salt marsh sediment and uptake of heavy metals by salt marsh species. *Proc. int. Conference on Heavy Metals in the Environment, Athens, Greece,* 545–547.

Salomons, W. & Eysink, W.D. 1981. Pathways of mud and particulate metals from rivers to the southern North sea. *Spec. Publs int. Assoc. Sedimentol.,* **5,** 429–450.

Salomons, W. & Förstner, U. 1984. *Metals in the hydrocycle.* Berlin: Springer. Berlin.

Simmers, J.W., Folsom, B.L., Lee, C.H.R. & Battes, D.J. 1981. Field survey of heavy metal uptake by naturally occurring salt water and fresh water marsh plants. *US Army Engineer Waterways Experiment Station, EL,* 81–85.

Smirnoff, N. & Crawford, R.M.M. 1983. Variation in the structure and response to flooding of root aerenchyma in some wetland plants. *Ann. Bot.,* **51,** 237–249.

Taylor, G.J. & Crowder, A.A. 1983. Uptake and accumulation of heavy metals by *Typha latifolia* L. in wetlands of Sudbury, Ontario region. *Can. J. Bot.,* **61,** 63–73.

Tessier, A., Campbell, P.G.C. & Bisson, M. 1979. Sequential extraction procedure for the specification of particulate trace metals. *Analyt. Chem.,* **51,** 844–851.

CHAPTER 11

Changes in the numbers of dunlin (*Calidris alpina*) in British estuaries in relation to changes in the abundance of *Spartina*

J D Goss-Custard[1] and M E Moser[2]

[1] *Institute of Terrestrial Ecology, Furzebrook Research Station, Wareham, Dorset, BH20 5AS*
[2] *British Trust for Ornithology, Beech Grove, Tring, Herts, HP23 5NR*

Summary

This study shows that the numbers of a small wading bird, the dunlin (*Calidris alpina*), wintering in British estuaries have declined since the early 1970s at the highest rates in estuaries where *Spartina* has spread by the greatest amount over the intertidal flats where the birds feed. Where the extent of *Spartina* has not changed at all, the numbers of dunlin have not declined significantly. However, dunlin numbers have not increased in those estuaries where *Spartina* has declined through natural dieback. Possible reasons are discussed.

1. Introduction

The spread of *Spartina* over intertidal flats has, for a number of years, been seen as a threat to the wading birds that winter on British estuaries. By physically preventing birds from entering an area, it is feared that dense stands of *Spartina* could remove a significant amount of the open flats on which most waders forage for their invertebrate prey. So strong has been the concern about the spread of *Spartina* in some wader feeding areas that attempts have been made to remove it (eg Corkhill 1982), even though there is no direct evidence that the grass is damaging to the birds.

Early indications that *Spartina* might be damaging to some waders were published in the proceedings of the last workshop on *Spartina* (Doody 1982). In that volume, Millard and Evans showed that waders were excluded by *Spartina* to varying degrees, the flocking dunlin being more affected than the more solitarily feeding redshank (*Tringa totanus*), which was still able to feed in the gaps between *Spartina* clumps. The main evidence that the numbers of waders might actually have been affected was given by Davis and Moss. They linked the rapid decline in numbers of several wader species on the Dyfi estuary during the 1970s with the very rapid expansion in *Spartina* that occurred there over the same period, but their study was restricted to one estuary. It was not possible to examine whether or not wader numbers had also decreased in other estuaries where *Spartina* had increased, or, indeed, whether bird numbers had increased where *Spartina* had declined. A more extensive survey was required to test this hypothesis.

This paper summarises the main findings of such a survey, the details of which are published elsewhere (Goss-Custard & Moser 1988). The study is restricted to populations of the dunlin wintering in Britain. These birds belong mainly to the race *alpina* (Hardy & Minton 1980) which breeds in northern Fenno-Scandinavia and the USSR, east to the River Kolyma (Cramp & Simmons 1983). They arrive in Britain from their breeding areas during autumn and winter, with peak numbers occurring during December and January (Prater 1981). Along with the other waders and wildfowl, they are counted in most British estuaries at monthly intervals by teams of ornithologists organised by the British Trust for Ornithology. The counts (Salmon & Moser 1985) show that, since the winter of 1971–72, when most estuaries were counted for the first time, the populations of most wader species wintering in Britain have either remained constant or increased. The dunlin is one of the few species whose numbers have declined, by almost 50% since the peak numbers recorded during the winter of 1973–74. However, the rates of change in dunlin numbers varied greatly between estuaries: in some, numbers hardly changed, whereas enormous decreases occurred in others. The aim of our survey was to test whether the rates of change in dunlin numbers in different estuaries were linked to the amount by which *Spartina* had increased or decreased its range.

2. Methods

Details of the methods used are given in Goss-Custard and Moser (1988). Basically, the winter peak in bird numbers for each estuary was plotted against the year, and the calculated regression coefficient used as a measure of the average rate of change in bird numbers over the period.

The change in extent to which *Spartina* had invaded or retreated on the intertidal flats during those years was estimated in three ways:

i. from published estimates of the area covered by *Spartina* at different times during the study period (data available from 11 estuaries);

ii. from the rankings, by three widely travelled experts, of the extent to which *Spartina* had decreased or increased in the ten most important estuaries for dunlin; and

iii. from local naturalists, who were asked whether *Spartina* had spread (or decreased), since 1971, by a large (scored 3), medium (2) or small (1) amount, or

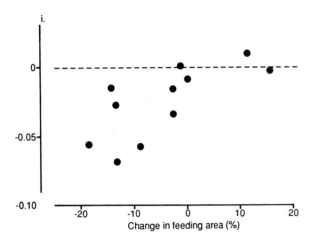

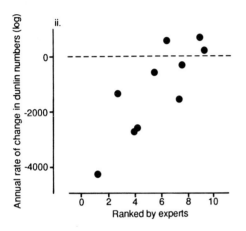

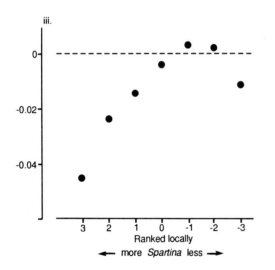

FIGURE 1. *The annual rate of change in dunlin numbers in three samples of estuaries*
i. Rates of change (logged bird numbers) for the period 1971–72 to 1985–86 in 11 estuaries plotted against the percentage of change in the area of intertidal flats available for the birds to use (rs=0.682, P < 0.05)
ii. Rates of change (untransformed counts) in the ten most important estuaries for dunlin against the ranked change in Spartina *abundance over the same period (1974–75 to 1984–85) (rs=0.723, P < 0.05). Dunlin data from Salmon and Moser (1985)*
iii. The mean annual rates of change in dunlin numbers (logged) in relation to the change in the abundance of Spartina *from 1971–72 to 1985–86*

not at all (0) (data from 60 estuaries, excluding 13 where some other factor seemed to have had an effect (Goss-Custard & Moser 1988).

All three methods for estimating the rates of change in abundance of *Spartina* were crude, but the differences between estuaries are so large that the methods should suffice. Most importantly, the measurements and judgements on *Spartina* were made without any knowledge of the change in dunlin numbers over the same period. There is no reason to think that the measures for *Spartina* were unconsciously biased according to the rate at which dunlin numbers had changed over the last 15 years.

3. Results

Whichever way was used to measure the increase or decrease in the extent of *Spartina*, dunlin numbers decreased at the greatest average annual rates in estuaries where *Spartina* had spread the most (Figure 1). (Note that the rates of change in dunlin numbers were calculated from logged bird numbers in Figures 1i and 1iii, whereas in Figure 1ii the untransformed counts were used). The numbers of birds using the various estuaries ranged from a few dozen individuals to 38 000, mainly according to the size of the estuary. By taking the logs of the bird counts, the proportionate rates of change on estuaries could be compared with very different population sizes. The untransformed data are shown in Figure 1ii to demonstrate that, in the worst affected estuary, dunlin numbers declined by an average of over 4000 per year during each of the ten years for which data for these estuaries are available.

Interestingly, the relationship appears to be curvilinear in all three analyses. Though dunlin numbers declined where *Spartina* spread, they did not increase where *Spartina* died back, even in the harbours of Poole and Langstone, where *Spartina* has decreased enormously during the period (Gray & Pearson 1982; Haynes 1982).

4. Discussion

The results show that dunlin numbers have decreased at the fastest rate in estuaries where *Spartina* has spread the most. This finding does not, however, necessarily prove a causal link. Dunlin numbers may have declined and *Spartina* spread for quite separate reasons. Alternatively, a change in another factor, such as shore level, may have affected both organisms independently. However, at Lindisfarne, dunlin moved back into areas that had been cleared of *Spartina* (Evans 1988), suggesting that the presence of the *Spartina* itself had affected the birds directly.

It is not difficult to envisage how the spread of *Spartina* might affect dunlin. In common with many waders, dunlin feed in winter for a very high proportion of the period during which the intertidal flats are exposed (Goss-Custard *et al.* 1977; Prater 1981), for the reason that, in winter, the food declines yet the birds' demand for it rises: Dunlin start feeding as soon as the higher mudflats are exposed on the receding tide, and continue almost without ceasing until the advancing tide covers the highest areas. Therefore, the spread of *Spartina* downshore not only reduces the area available for feeding, but also curtails the amount of time for which the birds can feed. This phenomenon could reduce numbers by deterring juveniles from settling in an estuary when they are prospecting for a place in which to spend the next and subsequent winters, and also by increasing the winter mortality rates of any birds that remain. Significantly, dunlin was one of the species most affected by the loss of upshore feeding areas at Teesmouth (Evans 1981; Prater 1981).

Yet why did dunlin numbers not increase in those estuaries where *Spartina* had receded since 1971? One explanation is that, when previously well-established *Spartina* recedes, it leaves the mudflats in an unsuitable condition for invertebrates to colonise. It is known that, at first, rapid erosion often occurs, leaving slumping platforms of mud and clay (Tubbs 1982) which may be unsuitable for invertebrates. In some places, thick algal mats have grown extensively over areas previously colonised by *Spartina*, and may provide unsuitable feeding areas for waders (Tubbs 1977). We need to examine these possibilities in more detail to see if they might explain the failure of dunlin numbers to increase where *Spartina* has died back naturally.

5. Acknowledgements

We are grateful to Drs A J Gray, M G Morris and R J O'Connor for commenting on the manuscript and to the many people, listed in Goss-Custard and Moser (1988), who provided information on *Spartina*.

The Birds of Estuaries Enquiry is organised by the British Trust for Ornithology and jointly sponsored by the BTO, Nature Conservancy Council and Royal Society for the Protection of Birds.

6. References

Corkhill, P. 1982. *Spartina* at Lindisfarne NNR and details of recent attempts to control its spread. In: Spartina anglica *in Great Britain*, edited by J.P. Doody, 60–63. (Focus on nature conservation no.5.) Attingham: Nature Conservancy Council.

Cramp, S. & Simmons, K.E.L. 1983. *Handbook of the birds of Europe, the Middle East and North Africa. The birds of the western Palaearctic*, 3. Oxford: Oxford University Press.

Davis, P. & Moss, D. 1982. *Spartina* and waders – the Dyfi estuary. In: Spartina anglica *in Great Britain*, edited by J.P. Doody, 37–40. (Focus on nature conservation no.5.) Attingham: Nature Conservancy Council.

Doody, P., ed. 1982. *Spartina anglica in Great Britain.* (Focus on nature conservation no.5.) Attingham: Nature Conservancy Council.

Evans, P.R. 1981. Reclamation of intertidal land: some effects on shelduck and wader populations in the Tees estuary. *Verh. orn. Ges. Bayern*, **23**, 147–168.

Evans, P.R. 1988. Use of the herbicide 'Dalapon' for control of *Spartina* encroaching on intertidal mudflats: beneficial effects on shorebirds. *Colonial Waterbirds*, **9**, 171–175.

Goss-Custard, J.D., Jenyon, R.A., Jones, R.E., Newberry, P.E. & Williams, R. Le B. 1977. The ecology of the Wash. II. Seasonal variation in the feeding conditions of wading birds (Charadrii). *J. appl. Ecol.*, **14**, 701–719.

Goss-Custard, J.D. & Moser, M.E. 1988. Rates of change in the numbers of dunlin *Calidris alpina* wintering in British estuaries in relation to the spread of *Spartina anglica*. *J. appl. Ecol.*, **25**, 95–109.

Gray, A.J. & Pearson, J.M. 1982. *Spartina* marshes in Poole Harbour, Dorset. In: Spartina anglica *in Great Britain*, edited by J.P. Doody, 11–14. (Focus on nature conservation no.5.) Attingham: Nature Conservancy Council.

Hardy, A.R. & Minton, C.D.T. 1980. Dunlin migration in Britain and Ireland. *Bird Study* **27**, 81–92.

Haynes, F.N. 1982. *Spartina* in Langstone Harbour, Hampshire. In: Spartina anglica *in Great Britain*, edited by J.P. Doody, 5–10. (Focus on nature conservation no.5.) Attingham: Nature Conservancy Council.

Millard, A.V. & Evans, P.R. 1982. Colonization of mudflats by *Spartina anglica*: some effects on invertebrate and shore bird populations at Lindisfarne. In: Spartina anglica *in Great Britain*, edited by J.P. Doody, 41–48. (Focus on nature conservation no.5.) Attingham: Nature Conservancy Council.

Prater, A.J. 1981. *Estuary birds of Britain and Ireland.* Calton: Poyser.

Salmon, D.G. & Moser, M.E. 1985. *Wildfowl and wader counts 1984–1985.* Slimbridge: Wildfowl Trust.

Tubbs, C. 1977. Wildfowl and waders in Langstone Harbour. *Br. Birds*, **70**, 177–199.

Tubbs, C. 1982. *Spartina* on the south coast: an introduction. In: Spartina anglica *in Great Britain*, edited by J.P. Doody, 3–4 (Focus on nature conservation no.5.) Attingham: Nature Conservancy Council.

CHAPTER 12

Twenty-five years of introduced *Spartina anglica* in China

Chung-Hsin Chung

Institute of Spartina and Tidal Land Studies, Nanjing University, Nanjing 210008, People's Republic of China

Summary

Introduced into China in 1963, *Spartina anglica* has been planted extensively and has spread to cover more than 36 000 ha ranging over 20° of latitude. This paper summarises the history of planting of the species, and describes the many uses of *Spartina*. Basic research on the plant's biology is also described briefly.

1. Introduction

Since *Spartina anglica* was first introduced to China in 1963, interest has been aroused in scientific circles in the western world. However, this paper provides the first comprehensive, summarised report, and is synthesised from both published and unpublished works.

2. Planting materials and planting

2.1 Sources of planting materials and their fates

Three batches were introduced in 1963: two from Mundon, Essex, England, and one collected in Hojer, Denmark. In 1964 and 1980, Dr D S Ranwell sent 18 plants from Poole Harbour and seeds collected from Lancashire. Out of 35 individuals in the first batch, only 21 survived, and their progeny has spread along almost the entire Chinese coast (except for a very small fringe of Poole Harbour-derived plants at very low elevations). The second consignment from Hojer dwindled, and a third, from Mundon, after being propagated to large numbers, was used for reclamation in Wenling County, Zhejiang; Lancashire plants have never been transplanted into intertidal zones.

2.2 Periods of plantings and development

Five periods may be delineated as follows.

i. Propagation and trial plantings – 1963–66
    Initial experiments were set up at the Xinyang Agricultural Station, Shenyang, Jiangsu (north of 35°N), and at our laboratory. Xinyang made a good start from July 1963 and after overwintering in glasshouses; a total of 435 000 individuals was obtained in 1964 (20 700 fold of 21!). At one time, it was the only supply centre of planting materials in China. At the end of 1963, Huanghua County, Hebei, south of Tianjin, began a programme of introductions from Xinyang and trial plantings. A number of visitors brought the plant to the north coast of Shandong and Dalian, Liaoning. Our venture, supported by scientists in Britain and the Netherlands, started in mid-February 1964, using Essex seeds. A station was established in Xiaoshan, south of the Chientang River, in late-April

1964, but accretion of 1 m depth wiped out the 0.2 ha plantation in August 1966. Other plantings were at Bogezhuang, Hebei, north of 39°N, and in seven counties of Fujian. The Wenling station was established at the end of 1964. The end of this period was marked by successful transplantations on intertidal land, 32 ha being planted by Xinyang and 78.33 by us.

ii. Very slow progress, 1966–73
     The 'Cultural Revolution' put an end to most trial plantings, although we, and a few others under our guidance, persisted. We planted 286.67 ha and Tianjin planted 33.33 ha. Several Zhejiang counties began trials under our advice. The end of this period was marked by the embankment of the first Chinese *Spartina* polder, after accretion of 80 cm in our plantation established in 1966–68 in Wenling. By this time, the total area planted was 12 000 ha.

iii. Resumption of work, 1973–78
      Characterised by the cultivation of crops in the first polder, work started in Jiangsu was extended to other provinces (eg Jiangsu and Shandong). A further 10 000 ha were planted by the end of this period.

iv. Climax development, 1978–80
     The National Committee of Science and Technology resumed direction of the project, and the Institute of *Spartina* and Tidal Land Development was established in 1978. Landmarks of this period were two nationwide meetings, held in Qidong and Wenling in 1978 and 1979, respectively. By the end of 1980, a planting area of 36 000 ha had been covered at varying densities. Previous experience was used to explore the use of these areas.

v. Studies of basic science and introduction of other species of *Spartina*, 1980–88
    In the last eight years, anatomical, cytological, physiological, biochemical, microbiological, zoological and plant geographical studies have been pursued. Taller species of *Spartina* (*S. alterniflora*, *S. patens* and *S. cynosuroides)* were introduced in 1977, and *S. pectinata* was imported very recently. Only *S. alterniflora* has become established, covering approximately 1300 ha in this country. New plantings of *S. anglica* have been made on a small scale for specific objectives.

2.3 Planting experiences

The success of the many planting schemes in Chinese provinces (arranged from north to south) is considered briefly below.

Negligible plantings were made in Liaoning Province prior to 1979, when a total area of 163 ha was planted in four cities and eleven counties. Survival generally ranged around 65%, with a maximum above 80%. Clump diameters varied from 20 cm to 50 cm, with 20–40 tillers per clump, and plants were between 20 cm and 40 cm tall. In later years, high mortalities occurred when temperatures suddenly fluctuated from +10°C to less than −10°C in spring.

In Hebei Province, 1960s plantings in Huanghua were destroyed by excessive accretion, but those in Bogezhuang still exist today. A further planting of 41.33 ha in Huanghua in 1978 was reduced to 18 ha, mainly by nereid damage and ice action, although 100% survival over 1.07 ha was achieved at Haikow Experimental Station. Of the 304.81 ha planted in 1979, about 140 ha survive, the sudden spring temperature fluctuations being the major reason for the losses.

Plantings began in Shandong in 1966, and in Showguang County, north of 37°N; 80% survival was attained by planting in holes and 20% by inserting in furrows. In later years, high survivorship was obtained, with rapid tillering and clump extension. Although the total area of plantings in the early 1980s was 3000 ha, it may have been reduced recently by cultivation.

Our work in Jiangsu Province started in the 1970s, and the planting area there has been the largest in China. New plantings totalled 2000 ha in 1977, 3333 ha in 1978, and 14 000 ha in 1979. Most of the 1960s work was done in Zhejiang Province, and here most experience of *Spartina* growth and propagation was gained (Chung *et al.* 1985). The effects of temperature were observed in Chientang River Farm, where growth was inhibited above 35°C and below 5°C. In particular, droughts during the exposed period from July to September led to poor performance, as did daily submergences over eight hours.

In Fujian, introductions in 1965 by seven counties were mostly neglected, but in 1979 in Fuding County (the northernmost county), north of 27°N, plantings of Wenling-derived grass in May were successful. After 130 days, clumps at 50 cm spacings had expanded from three to an average of 156 tillers. North of 25°N, two planting seasons were distinguished: March to June and late-August to end-October. The intense heat of July depressed survival considerably, with very slow coalescing of clumps.

In Guangdong Province, plantings were made in Dianbei in 1974, and growth was exceptionally good, with individuals up to 70 cm tall and rhizomes growing up to 110 cm from April to September. One individual, planted in April, produced 353 tillers in a 60 cm diameter clump and had amassed 2.5 kg of fresh weight by the end of October. A small number of plants from Dianbei were tried in Guangxi Province before Wenling plants were introduced there in 1979. Survival was low (30%) because of the two-week journey. One nursery did succeed by good management and fertilisation, producing generally dense stands, but another failed because of poor irrigation methods, an acid reclamation soil, and poor-quality planting material.

2.4 General results

The geographical distribution of *Spartina anglica* ranges from our northernmost county, Panshan, Liaoning, 40°53'N, to Dianbei, Guangdong, 21°27'N (south of the Tropic of Cancer). The plant survived for several months in Haikow, Hainan Island, at 20°02'N, where it was killed by a sudden drainage problem (Chung 1983b).

Remarkably, vast areas of *Spartina* plantations have been derived from 21 individuals. Propagation from seeds was begun in mid-February 1964, 44 seedlings being replicated to obtain 30 600 individual tillers by April 1965. Young seedlings did not begin tillering until five or six leaves had been formed, and grew best in pots without drainage. Propagation from rhizomes took two years and four months, namely 375 days in pots and 475 days of paddy cultures, but this method produced about 9 100 000 plants, and formed the largest plantation in China in the 1960s. However, only 30 ha of the 286.67 ha were from these plants, the rest being occupied by the progeny of four individuals of 15 June 1964.

Under adequate water supply, *S. anglica* survived air temperatures of 40.5–42.0°C for eight consecutive days in July 1964, and was able to overwinter safely at very low temperatures. Minimum winter temperatures recorded at *S. anglica* sites include −8°C (Huanghua County, Hebei, 1964–65), −11.3°C (Shenyang, 1963–64), −14.5°C (Tianjin, 1965–66) and −22°C (Qinhuangdao, a little south of 40°N, in 1966–67). Fresh green culms and leaves were seen under ice in Tianjin in early February 1965, and even in Panshan, its northernmost station, luxuriant summer growth has been proof of safe overwintering.

The species is able to withstand great extremes of tidal submergence and sediment accretion. Continuous submergence for over 70 hours was observed in a muddy inland tidal creek, and accretion rates as high as 80 cm in three years (at Rudong salt flat) and 93 cm in four years (at Qidong) (Cao & Zhuo 1985) were observed. This ability has made the plant a useful coastline stabilising agent, even in high wave energy conditions.

It is a good agent of amelioration not only for saline soil but also for alkaline soil (Ou *et al.* 1982, 1985), even where irrigated with underground saline water (Liu & Yiao 1985, 1987) and in areas of infertile embanked soil (Chung *et al.* 1985). It is also highly tolerant of heavy metals, such as mercury (Chung & Qin 1938, 1985), caesium, strontium, cadmium and zinc (Wang *et al.* 1985). It has provided a new source of green manure, animal fodder, fish feed and the raw materials of paper and rope-making (see below).

3. Uses

3.1 Accretion for reclamation

Annual sedimentation rates in *Spartina anglica* zones in most coastal provinces varied from 3.3 cm to 19.0 cm. Levels in the centre of the clump were sometimes 19 cm higher than at its periphery after two-and-a-half years (Chung 1985). Accretion, reclamation, land use and the cultivation of crops have been summarised elsewhere (Chung *et al.* 1985).

3.2 Amelioration of saline soils

Although *Spartina* marsh soil contained more salts than unvegetated mudflat soil, it rapidly desalinised after embankment and ploughing. High soil fertility was reported to result from the accumulation of vast quantities of below-ground biomass, higher granulation of soil particles, greater porosity and aeration, and less soil bulk density. In the arid north of China, inland irrigation with saline groundwater resulted in a decrease of soil salinity and an increase of nutrients (Liu & Yiao 1985, 1987).

The accumulation of organic matter in soils below *Spartina anglica* was compared with that below other marsh plants. The percentages in *S. anglica* areas were 0.73, 1.03 and 1.30, after one, three and six years, respectively. By contrast, in two years from barren mudflat to *Suaeda salsa* stage, 0.33–0.5% of organic matter accumulated, with 0.51–0.60% in the stage from *Suaeda* to *Aeluropus littoralis* var. *sinensis* (10–15 years) and 0.6–0.87% from the latter to *Imperata cylindrica* (8–10 years).

3.3 Coastline stabilisation

S. anglica has a below- to above-ground ratio of around 4:1, and the network of roots and rhizomes binds the soil particles, while the culms and leaves trap suspended sediments (Chung 1982). Following communications from Lianyunggang, we were encouraged to turve the face of an earth sea wall in Qidong with *Spartina* sods. A 380 m^2 experimental area remained intact following a typhoon attack, with windspeeds of 28 m s^{-1}. (Cao & Zhuo 1985). It withstood a more severe typhoon in 1981, during which, by contrast, 10–15 cm of soil was scoured from unvegetated salt flats. The labour of repairing sea banks in some parts of Qidong has been saved, to the relief of many people.

3.4 Green manure

Spartina has been employed as a new source of green manure, especially indispensible for late crops of rice. At present (at least until a few years ago), 75% of the 8965 ha standing crop of *Spartina* plantations in Wenling is used for this purpose. As winter-green manure crops are used up for early rice crops, there is a shortage of summer-green manure, and its importance has been unanimously recognised. In the late-1960s,

farmers preferred *S. anglica* manure for its longer effect, for improving soil structure, and for introducing fewer weeds to rice paddies. Inland farmers traded it with chemical fertilisers. Net increases in yield of late rice crops ranged from 750 to 1125 kg ha^{-1} in inland farms, and from 452.5 to 677.25 kg ha^{-1} in coastal farms; 100 kg of *Spartina* grass was evaluated as being equivalent in fertility to one kg of urea, and a little higher than that of an equal amount of pig manure. The net increase in yield of the late rice crop from 1978 to 1984 was estimated to be at least 2 570 000 kg.

3.5 Pasture land and use as animal fodder

The establishment of the first Chinese *Spartina* marsh pasture land in Qidong in 1976 quickly revealed the many advantages of such a system. These advantages include the rapid creation of a grazing marsh with a high production of fresh grass (1729 kg for a single harvest and 2124 kg in two harvests) and a high carrying capacity, about 0.2 ha being needed to support a single sheep or goat (visitors were highly impressed by this fact). *Spartina* has a relatively high palatability (even in winter, with partially greenish grass eagerly devoured by both sheep and goats) and high digestibility (68.86% tested with a man-made rumen). Animals grazing on such marshes are generally healthy and receive sufficient mineral nutrients by daily tides, without the deficiency in certain microelements found in some inland grasslands. There is also a saving of manpower on *Spartina* pastures.

Domestic animals fed on *Spartina* include mules, pigs, cattle, buffalo, dairy cows, goats, dairy goats, sheep, rabbits, geese, and even large-sized animals such as donkeys and horses. In Wenling, Chinese wild geese abandoned wheat fields for the newly established *Spartina* marsh. A *Spartina* plantation of about 2 ha was almost destroyed by wild geese, even the rhizomes being plucked up from the soil!

Shandong School of Veterinary Medicine and Animal Husbandry conducted feeding experiments with the following results.

Kinds of animals	Heads fed by minimum yield	Heads fed by maximum yield
Ewe	1.57	23.55
Western Shandong cattle	0.15–2.25	5.85
Beef or dairy cattle (500 kg weight)	1.80	4.65
Rabbits	58.5	156.75
Grass geese	175.8	470.4

Laoshan County of Greater Qingdao has analysed two important components of feeding value, *viz* crude protein (±13%) and crude celluloses (21%). These values compare favourably with those of such crops as corn, rice and soybean straw, as well as rice bran, sweet potato vines and others. Protein, fat, cellulose, carotin and minerals of Qidong plants have been analysed by Lu and Jiang (1981, 1985). Silage has been made successfully at Qinhuangdao, Zhenhai, Wenling and Showguang.

3.6 *Fish feed*

The first venture was started by a commune in Qidong, which bought and transported 1200 kg fresh *Spartina* grass daily to feel tilapia, Chinese grass carp, and other fish. In 1983, I visited a new fishery which had covered 45 ha of reclaimed *Spartina* in Qidong, and took the opportunity actually to see *Spartina* grass being cut on the marsh. From this enterprise, 125 000 kg of fish fed with *Spartina* were supplied to big cities. Experiments in fish production and utilisation occurred in Haiyiang County, northern Zheijiang, and at the Cyanzhou Fishery, with favourable results.

3.7 *Increased production of nereids and other animals*

Six hundred ha of *Spartina* marshes in Wenling and 300 ha in Yühuan were destroyed in 1981 to obtain nereids for sale to export agencies (Chung 1983b). In a sample of 215 m² quadrats, a survey in Yühuan showed increased numbers of nereids in *Spartina* marsh as opposed to unvegetated salt flats (a mean of 7.4 g *vs* 0.8 g and 10.1 g *vs* 0.77 g in body weight). In further samples, sand crabs (4 *vs* 2) and molluscs (685 *vs* 18) were also found to occur in higher numbers in the marsh.

3.8 *Use as fuel and raw materials for paper-making*

Generation of marsh gas began in Wenling in the late-1970s, and in 1984 20% of the *Spartina* standing crop was used as fuel, including raw materials for generating marsh gas. Brown, unbleached paper has been manufactured by the Dongfang commune since 1968.

4. *Basic scientific studies*

A wide range of studies on the anatomy, morphology, cytology, physiology and biochemistry of *Spartina anglica* has been conducted in China.

Zhou and Chung (1985a) have examined seed morphology in relation to germination, and Wang *et al.* (1979) have confirmed the anatomical findings of Long, Incoll and Woolhouse (1975), using optical and scanning electron microscopy. They distinguished two types of chloroplasts: those in the mesophyll, which were 4.5 μ in diameter, and those in the vascular bundle sheath cells, which were 7.6 μ. Chloroplasts were more abundant in sheath cells. Culm and leaf sheaths were studied, revealing vascular bundles arranged in three circles. Stomata were found on both adaxial and abaxial sides, but salt glands only on the abaxial (Sung & Dou 1982, 1985). Root hairs were discovered on secondary adventitious roots and on side roots (Wang & Dou 1985). Dense cytoplasm, large nucleoli, numerous mitochondria and a few other organelles of both cap

and basal cells of salt glands were investigated (Zhou, Jiang & Dou 1982; Zhou *et al.* 1985). Jiang and Huang (1982, 1985) have developed and improved methods of preserving membranous systems, nucleoli and lipid droplets with digallic acid-treated materials.

The chromosome number was determined as 2n=116 instead of 2n=122, as found by Marchant (1968) (Fang *et al.* 1982). Lü and Lu (1985) developed a method of purifying DNA in the seedlings of *S. anglica* without organic solvents or enzymes and without using high-speed centrifuges. DNA was successfully transferred to rice, and experiments on protein, amino acid, and morphological changes were made for seven generations (Chen & Duan 1985).

A four-year study in which plants of different stature were grown in our botanic garden indicated that tall and short forms were ecophenes rather than ecotypes, although one 'tall form' persisted (Zhuo *et al.* unpublished). The three populations from Essex, Poole Harbour and Lancashire were thought to be ecotypes, showing differences in the ultrastructure of leaf cells, in proline accumulation, and in the banding patterns of two iso-enzymes under stress conditions. The Lancashire population has been defined as a low-temperature, salt-tolerant ecotype, that from Essex as a low-temperature, low salt-tolerant ecotype, and the Poole Harbour population as a high-temperature, salt-tolerant ecotype (Zhuang & Chung unpublished).

The physiology and biochemistry of both seed and whole plants have been studied. Seed storage and germination experiments showed that germination occurred only after wet storage at low temperature (5°C): germination rates were 3.7% after one day, with a continuous increase of up to 61.7% after 26 days, and no increase after that. The optimum conditions were at 25°C in a dark room (Lü, Shen & Chung 1984, 1985). Germination rates have been increased by puncturing seeds to eliminate inhibition in endosperm (Zhou & Chung 1985b) and by reducing atmospheric pressure (Zhang *et al.* 1985). Excised embryos showed complete germination within a week, in contrast to dormant seeds without excision of endosperms which showed no sign of germination three weeks later.

The alkaline tolerance of *Spartina* has been investigated by Ou and colleagues (Ou *et al.* 1982, 1985).

Zhang *et al.* (1985) studied proline accumulation, which was generally much lower than in England (Stewart & Lee 1974). Proline content in seedlings cultured in distilled water varied little with age, but those cultured in seawater contained a higher quantity, and proline content was found to be closely related to external sodium chloride (NaCl) concentrations (Lü & Chung 1982a, b). Although proline accumulated gradually as root external NaCl concentrations reached 0.2 M, at 0.5 M NaCl solution the proline contents of leaves and stems increased rapidly for 24–36 hours, after which a rise was no longer noted (Lu & Jiang 1982, 1985).

Other research has ranged from computer-based numerical taxonomic studies of the Gram negative bacteria isolated from the plant surfaces of *S. anglica* (Zhou *et al.* 1985) through surveys of the distribution of animals in *Spartina* plantations (Tong, Meng & Xü 1985), to studies of decomposition and production (Jiang *et al.* 1987).

5. References

Cao, H. & Zhuo, R.Z. 1985. A study of synecology and productivity of *Spartina anglica* plantation in Qidong County, Jiangsu. *J. Nanjing Univ. Res. Adv. Spartina*, 83–115.

Chen, S.B. & Duan, X.L. 1985. Character changes induced by transfer of DNA into rice. *Scientia Agricultura Sinica*, **3**, 6–9.

Chung, C.H. 1982. Low marsh, China. In: *Creation and restoration of coastal plant communities*, edited by R.R. Lewis, 131–145. Boca Raton, Fl: CRC Press.

Chung, C.H. 1983a. Introduction of *Spartina anglica* to China and its utilisation. *Natural Resources (Beijing)*, **1**, 45–50.

Chung, C.H. 1983b. Geographical distribution of *Spartina anglica* Hubbard in China. *Bull. Mar. Sci. (Miami)*, **33**, 753–758.

Chung C.H. 1985. Effects of introduced *Spartina* grass on coastal morphology in China. *Z. Geomorph. N.F.*, Suppl.-Band **57**, 169–174.

Chung, C.H. & Qin, P. 1983. An enquiry into the mercury absorption by *Spartina anglica* and its environmental purification effect. *Mar. Sci. (Qingdao)*, **2(6)**, 6–11.

Chung, C.H. & Qin, P. 1985. Absorption of mercury by *Spartina anglica* and its purification effect. *Collected Oceanic Works* (Tianjin, all in English), **1**, 24–33.

Chung (Zhong), C.H., Zhuo, R.Z., Zhou, H.B., Ye, G.H., Hu, C.H., Yin, B.Y., Jin, L.Z. & Pan, X.L. 1985. Experiments of trial plantings of *Spartina anglica* Hubbard and effects of saline soil amelioration in China. *J. Nanjing Univ. Res. Adv. Spartina*, 44–82.

Fang, T.S., Ho, J.L., Zhou, R.L., Dai, I.X. & Lin, G.H. 1982. The chromosome numbers of *Spartina anglica* and *S. patens*. *J. Shandong Coll. Oceanology*, **12(1)**, 65–68.

Jiang, H.X. & Huang, J.S. 1982. The preliminary observations on the digallic acid-treated transmission of electron microscopic specimens of *S. anglica* C.E. Hubbard. *J. Cell. Biol. (Shanghai)*, **4(2)**, 15–16.

Jiang, H.X. & Huang, J.S. 1985. Abstract. *J. Nanjing Univ. Res. Adv. Spartina*, 334–335.

Jiang, F.X., Wang, W.Z., Zhao, M. & Chung, C.H. 1987. A preliminary study of two species of *Spartina* decomposition and nutrient composition. *Acta Oceanographia Sinica*, **9(3)**, 367–371.

Liu, C.H. & Yiao, Y.H. 1985. First interim report on amelioration of saline soil by irrigating *Spartina anglica* with saline underground water. *J. Nanjing Univ. Res. Adv. Spartina*, 324–325.

Liu, C.H. & Yiao, Y.H. 1987. Experimental investigation on inland saline soil by means of *Spartina anglica* plantings. *Bot. Bull. (Beijing)*. In press.

Long, S.P., Incoll, L.D. & Woolhouse, H.W. 1975. C⁴ photosynthesis in plants from cool temperate regions, with particular reference to *Spartina townsendii*. *Nature, Lond.*, **257**, 622–624.

Lu, B.S. & Jiang, F.X. 1981. Studies on the nutritive value of *Spartina anglica*. *J. Nanjing Univ. (Nat. Sci.)*, **4**, 531–536; Abstract. *J. Nanjing Univ. Res. Adv. Spartina* (1985), 342–343.

Lu, B.S. & Jiang, F.X. 1982. The accumulation of free proline in *Spartina anglica* under saline conditions. *J. Nanjing Univ. (Nat. Sci.)*, **4**, 895–900.

Lu, B.S. & Jiang, F.X. 1985. Abstract. *J. Nanjing Univ. Res. Adv. Spartina*, 344–345.

Lü, H.M. & Lu, B.S. 1985. Purification and identification of DNA in seedlings of *Spartina anglica* Hubbard. *J. Nanjing Univ. Res. Adv. Spartina*, 351.

Lü, Z.X. & Chung, C.H. 1982a. The influence of NaCl on free amino acid composition and proline content of *Spartina anglica* seedlings. *Acta Phytophysiologia Sinica (Shanghai)*, **8(4)**, 393–396; Abstract. (1985). *J. Nanjing Univ. Res. Adv. Spartina*, 347.

Lü, Z.X. & Chung, C.H. 1982b. A comparative study of amino acid composition and proline content of *Spartina anglica* seedlings grown in fresh and sea water conditions. *J. Nanjing Univ. Res. Adv. Spartina*, 334–335.

Lü, Z.X., Shen, H.G. & Chung, C.H. 1984. The effect of storage methods on germination of *Spartina anglica* seeds. *J. Nanjing Univ. (Nat. Sci.)*, **1**, 127–133.

Lü, Z.X., Shen, H.G. & Chung, C.H. 1985. Abstract. *J. Nanjing Univ. Res. Adv. Spartina*, 336–337.

Marchant, C.J. 1968. Evolution in *Spartina* (Gramineae). II. Chromosomes, basic relationships and the problem of *Spartina townsendii* agg. *J. Linn. Soc. Bot.*, **60**, 381–409.

Ou, H.C., Fu, T.Z., Que, R.S. & Chung, C.H. 1982. A preliminary study of tolerance to alkalinity and salinity by seedlings of *Spartina anglica* Hubbard. *Plant Physiological Communications (Shanghai)*, 36–38; Abstract. (1985). *J. Nanjing Univ. Res. Adv. Spartina*, 338–339.

Ou, H.C., Fu, T.Z., Zhou, A.T., Yin, B., Chung, C.H. & Que, R.S. 1985. Biological basis of long time establishment of *Spartina anglica* in alkaline soil. *J. Nanjing Univ. Res. Adv. Spartina*, 179–184.

Stewart, G.R. & Lee, J.A. 1974. The role of proline accumulation in halophytes. *Planta (Berl.)*, **120**, 279–289.

Sung, R.J. & Dou, R.L. 1982. Biological characteristics of *Spartina anglica*. II. The structure of the culm and the leaf sheath. *J. Nanjing Univ. (Nat. Sci.)*, **1**, 111–116.

Sung, R.J. & Dou, R.L. 1985. Abstract. *J. Nanjing Univ. Res. Adv. Spartina*, 331.

Tong, Y.R., Meng, W.X. & Xü, Q. 1985. A preliminary survey of animals in *Spartina anglica* marsh. *J. Nanjing Univ. Res. Adv. Spartina*, 133–140.

Wang, B.K., Zhou, A.H., Wang, X.R., Zhou, D., Zhang, Z.R. & Pan, D.M. 1985. Accumulation and distribution of radioisotopes ¹²⁷Cs, ⁹⁰Sr, ¹¹⁵mCd and ⁶⁵Zn in *Spartina anglica*. *J. Nanjing Univ. Res. Adv. Spartina*, 124–132.

Wang, H.J. & Dou, R.L. 1985. Biological characteristics of *Spartina anglica* III. Anatomy of root system. *J. Nanjing Univ. Res. Adv. Spartina*, 149–158.

Wang, H.J., Zhou, H.B., Sung, R.J., Jiang, H.X. & Chen, L. 1979. Biological characteristics of *Spartina anglica*. I. Preliminary observation on the structure of the leaf. *J. Nanjing Univ. (Nat. Sci.)*, **3**, 45–52.

Zhang, C.G., Zhou, H.S., Wang, C.H. & Yuan, Y.S. 1985. Preliminary analysis on amino acid pool and total amino acids of *Spartina anglica* Hubbard. *J. Nanjing Univ. Res. Adv. Spartina*, 206–211.

Zheng, J.S., Ye, R.X., Ou, H.C., Fu, T.Z. & Zhang, Z.R. 1985. The effect of atmospheric pressure to seed germination of *Spartina anglica*. *J. Nanjing Univ. Res. Adv. Spartina*, 171–178.

Zhou, H.B. & Chung, C.H. 1985a. An enquiry on seed germination of *Spartina anglica*. I. Seed morphology in relation to germination. *J. Nanjing Univ. Res. Adv. Spartina*, 159–165.

Zhou, H.B. & Chung, C.H. 1985b. An enquiry on seed germination of *Spartina anglica*. II. The relationship between puncture of seeds and germination. *J. Nanjing Univ. Res. Adv. Spartina*, 166–170.

Zhou, H.B., Jiang, H.X. & Dou, R.L. 1982. Morphology of salt gland of *Spartina anglica* Hubbard. *Acta Botanica Sinica*, **24(2)**, 115–119; Abstract. (1985). *J. Nanjing Univ. Res. Adv. Spartina*, 332–333.

Zhou, H.L., Wang, Z.F., Cao, Y.Q. & Yü, W.H. 1985. Numerical taxonomic studies on the Gram negative bacteria isolated from the plant surface of *Spartina anglica* C.E. Hubbard. *J. Nanjing Univ. Res. Adv. Spartina*, 141–148.

CHAPTER 13

Spartina – friend or foe? A conservation viewpoint

J P Doody

Nature Conservancy Council, Northminster House, Peterborough, PE1 1UA

Summary

Spartina anglica has had both beneficial and harmful effects on salt marshes in Britain. Among the benefits are the prevention of coastal erosion, the increase in estuarine productivity, and the creation of grazing marsh through succession. Those effects which can be considered harmful to nature conservation interests include the invasion of wader and wildfowl feeding grounds, the replacement of a more diverse pioneer plant community, and the production of monospecific swards which are in some areas themselves replaced by swards of single species, such as *Phragmites australis* and *Scirpus maritimus*. This overall reduction in diversity, both plant and animal, means that, on balance, *Spartina* decreases the nature conservation value of those estuaries it invades, and that it should be eliminated or controlled in sites of high wildlife interest.

1. Introduction

The origin, history and spread of *Spartina anglica* (hereafter called *Spartina*) have been outlined in this volume and elsewhere (Marchant 1967; Hubbard & Stebbings 1967; Doody 1984). This paper considers the impact of the species on our native salt marsh vegetation and on the intertidal flats to seaward. In order to assess its effect on nature conservation interest, it is important to consider the attributes of the species which have made it so successful as a pioneer. The most significant are:

– its ability rapidly to colonise intertidal flats and mudflats, through extensive seedling establishment;

– its high productivity and growth rate (Long & Mason 1983);

– its ability to trap fine sediments and stabilise mudflats, and to produce monospecific swards in a relative short timescale.

The history and spread of *Spartina* may be summarised briefly.

1. A rapid expansion in the south of England (Tubbs 1984) between 1870 and 1923, followed by south-east and east England. Evidence of regression in this geographical area has subsequently been chronicled for several estuaries, including Langstone Harbour (Haynes 1984) and Poole Harbour (Gray & Pearson 1984).

2. A further rapid expansion in recent years to Wales and to north-west and north-east England (Deadman 1984).

3. Limited extension of its range in Scotland by a slow expansion of individual colonies through vegetative growth (Smith 1982).

The rapid expansion of the species in England and Wales, which has been documented in the references given above, was aided by its introduction at most of the sites by man. The reasons for these introductions provide us with some of the answers to the question posed in this paper – is *Spartina* 'friend' or 'foe'?

2. *Spartina* as a 'friend'

The use of the species as a 'land reclaiming agent' was probably first suggested in 1907 by Lord Montagu of Beaulieu to the Royal Commission on Coast Erosion (Stapf 1913). Since then, many of the introductions to estuaries in Great Britain have been aimed at 'stabilisation, coast protection and reclamation' (Ranwell 1967). The rôle of salt marsh in general, and *Spartina* in particular, in relation to stabilisation and protection of the coast has been considered recently at a conference of river engineers, held at Crowfield in 1984 (Randerson 1984). Examples of marsh enclosure, particularly for agricultural reclamation, can be seen at many places around the British coast, notably in Essex and Kent, where some 4000 ha have been 'won' from the sea. More recent examples of relatively large-scale development are those which have taken place in the Wash, at Cockerham and Pilling Marsh in Lancashire, and on the Ribble estuary.

Spartina is also a highly productive species and may contribute a considerable amount of organic material to the estuarine ecosystem (Long *et al.*, p34). This contribution may be a very important part of the primary productivity which provides the basis for the large numbers of invertebrate animals of the mudflats and their predators – the wintering wader population. Evidence from north Wales indicates that the expanding edge of an actively growing *Spartina* marsh is important as a nursery for bass (*Dicentrarchus labrax*).

Quite extensive areas of salt marsh are used for grazing animals, notably in north-west England. *Spartina* is reasonably palatable, particularly for the older breeds of sheep, and there are a few sites today where it is grazed, eg Bridgwater Bay in Somerset and Traeth Bach in Gwynedd. However, it is the flat lawns dominated by *Puccinellia maritima* and *Festuca rubra* which provide the most palatable grazing, and extensive use is made of these in the north and west for cattle and sheep. Such marshes may develop from *Spartina* marsh, particularly when the latter are grazed, as in Bridgwater Bay (Ranwell 1964) and on the Ribble estuary.

In Britain, there have been few other economic uses for *Spartina*, although silage was successfully produced in experiments in Bridgwater Bay (Hubbard & Ranwell

1966). Indeed, *Spartina* has become the object of much experimental and research interest, and in that sense has a certain value.

In summary, the attributes of *Spartina* which may be regarded as beneficial (and may not necessarily conflict with nature conservation interests) are:

- its rôle in preventing coastal erosion and stabilising mudflats;

- its use as an aid to reclamation, most importantly for agriculture;

- its high productivity, of possible value to the estuarine ecosystem;

- the creation, via succession, of grazing marsh;

- its value for research.

3. Spartina as a foe?

It is largely through its impact on the native salt marsh flora and the mudflat fauna that *Spartina* may be considered to be a foe. Even in the very early days when *Spartina* was thought of as a great aid to stabilisation and reclamation, many of the reports identified problems. Stapf (1913) cites 'interesting economic effects in the fauna', including the loss of large molluscs which were collected for food. Other reports of its invasion of the mudflats refer to the replacement of *Zostera* beds (Oliver 1925; Chapman 1959). Ranwell and Downing (1960) consider the decline in *Zostera* to be caused by a 'wasting disease', which was further aggravated by the rapid spread of *Spartina*. Many estuaries appear to have a relatively stable low water mark, eg the Solent (Tubbs 1980). In others, particularly those with deep river channels and steeply shelving shorelines, there is little scope for further accretion of the intertidal flats. This effectively means that, as *Spartina* invades these areas, there is an overall loss of open sand and mudflat habitat.

Such habitats support the large populations of invertebrate animals which are prey for wintering wildfowl and wader species, whose numbers may attain international significance. Pressure on this habitat, particularly from reclamation both of the flats directly and through the extension of salt marsh (often in front of a previous reclamation), is prevalent throughout Great Britain. Such pressure results in a cumulative loss of the habitat and increases the difficulty faced by birds in obtaining sufficient food (including *Zostera* for herbivores such as the Brent goose (*Branta bernicla*)). This difficulty may be particularly severe in periods of bad weather or when the birds arrive in Britain following their autumn migration.

Evidence that *Spartina* is having a significant effect on wader populations is beginning to mount. Goss-Custard and Moser (p69) discuss the relationship between the decline in dunlin (*Calidris alpina*) numbers and the spread of *Spartina* in several British estuaries. On a local scale, in Wader Bay in the Dyfi estuary, although

Spartina has invaded only about 10% of the intertidal flats, this invasion has been at the expense of some of the most favoured wader feeding sites (Davis & Moss 1984). The loss of intertidal feeding areas and the steepening of the beach profile are also thought to be a potential threat to bird populations at Lindisfarne NNR (Millard & Evans 1984). The obvious reduction in feeding areas that occurs as *Spartina* invades the flats has prompted such control measures as have taken place, notably at Lindisfarne NNR, Northumberland, the Dyfi estuary, and the Cefni estuary, Anglesey.

Botanically, the effect of *Spartina* on the native flora is clear. Because of its obvious ability to replace the natural pioneer plants, including *Puccinellia maritima*, *Salicornia europaea* and *Suaeda maritima*, the course of succession is irreversibly altered. On the south coast, extensive, largely monospecific swards have developed, containing little interest for nature conservation. On the west coast, two forms of succession appear to have taken place. On grazed marshes the sward is being replaced by *Puccinellia*, but in ungrazed *Spartina* marsh stands of *Phragmites australis* and/or *Scirpus maritimus* occur at the upper levels (as recorded for Bridgwater Bay by Ranwell (1964)). Both the latter species produce plant communities which are much impoverished in comparison with those which normally develop at this level. The rapidity of succession undoubtedly prevents other plant species being able to compete and invade such swards, which are also devoid of diverse animal communities.

An indirect effect of *Spartina* is that, by encouraging coastal land reclamation for agriculture, it leads to a loss of species-rich upper salt marshes together with their associated fauna, including breeding birds and terrestrial invertebrates. Such marshes are frequently those destroyed by land reclamation schemes, as around the Wash.

In summary, *Spartina* may be regarded as harmful to nature conservation interests by:

- invading intertidal flats which are rich in invertebrates and are the feeding grounds of large numbers of overwintering waders and wildfowl;

- replacing a potentially more diverse pioneer plant community;

- producing dense, monospecific swards which change the course and pace of succession and are replaced, in ungrazed areas, by tall communities equally poor in species;

- by promoting the reclamation of land for agriculture, thus destroying species-rich, high-level salt marsh.

4. Conclusions

Spartina anglica has greatly accelerated the rate of growth and total area of salt marsh in Great Britain, which, in turn, has aided the process of salt marsh enclosure for reclamation for a variety of uses, including agricultural land. The loss of salt marsh and the cumulative loss of intertidal sand and mudflats have probably had the most significant impact on nature conservation interests.

The attributes that make *Spartina* such a good species for the stabilisation of mudflats are also those which prevent it providing anything other than a reduced value for nature conservation. Despite its value in protecting high-level salt marsh, and its contribution to the estuarine food chain, the overall conclusion must be that, at present, *Spartina* provides a threat in estuaries of high wildlife interest, both to bird populations and to natural salt marsh succession.

As with most species which can rapidly invade open habitats, once established *Spartina* is difficult to eradicate. Problems will be more effectively avoided if the species is controlled when it first appears, rather than waiting until it becomes a problem. This is particularly important in estuaries of high wildlife interest. Of course, this approach may create a conflict between the need to protect shorelines and the needs of nature conservation. At some sites, the only practical solution to resolve this conflict, and on grounds of cost, may be to carry out a continual programme of control along the expanding edge of the marsh. Such a programme requires monitoring the expansion in individual sites in order to identify those areas that require treatment.

5. References

Chapman, V.J. 1959. Studies in saltmarsh ecology. IX. Changes in saltmarsh vegetation at Scolt Head Island. *J. Ecol.,* **47,** 619–639.

Davis, P. & Moss, D. 1984. *Spartina* and waders – the Dyfi estuary. In: Spartina anglica *in Great Britain,* edited by J.P. Doody, 37–40. (Focus on nature conservation no.5.) Attingham: Nature Conservancy Council.

Deadman, A. 1984. Recent history of *Spartina* in north west England and in north Wales and its possible future development. In: Spartina anglica *in Great Britain,* edited by J.P. Doody, 22–24. (Focus on nature conservation no. 5.) Attingham: Nature Conservancy Council.

Doody, J.P., ed. 1984. Spartina anglica *in Great Britain.* (Focus on nature conservation no. 5.) Attingham: Nature Conservancy Council.

Gray, A.J. & Pearson, J.M. 1984. *Spartina* marshes in Poole Harbour, Dorset with particular reference to Holes Bay. In: Spartina anglica *in Great Britain,* edited by J.P. Doody, 11–14. (Focus on nature conservation no. 5.) Attingham: Nature Conservancy Council.

Haynes, F.N. 1984. *Spartina* in Langstone Harbour, Hampshire. In: Spartina anglica *in Great Britain,* edited by J.P. Doody, 5–10. (Focus on nature conservation no. 5.) Attingham: Nature Conservancy Council.

Hubbard, J.C.E. & Ranwell, D.S. 1966. Cropping *Spartina* saltmarsh for silage. *J. Br. Grassld Soc.,* **21,** 214–217.

Hubbard, J.C.E. & Stebbings, R.E. 1967. Distribution, dates of origin and acreage of *Spartina townsendii (s.l.)* marshes in Great Britain. *Trans. bot. Soc. Br. Isl.,* **7,** 1–7.

Long, S.P. & Mason, C.F. 1983. *Saltmarsh ecology.* Glasgow: Blackie.

Marchant, C.J. 1967. Evolution in *Spartina* (Gramineae). I. The history and morphology of the genus in Britain. *J. Linn. Soc. Bot.,* **60,** 1–24.

Millard, A.V. & Evans, P.R. 1984. Colonisation of mudflats by *Spartina anglica;* some effects on invertebrates and shore bird populations at Lindisfarne. In: Spartina anglica *in Great Britain,* edited by J.P. Doody, 41–48. (Focus on nature conservation no. 5.) Attingham: Nature Conservancy Council.

Oliver, F.W. 1925. *Spartina townsendii:* its modes of establishment, economic uses and taxonomic status. *J. Ecol.,* **13,** 74–91.

Randerson, P.F. 1984. *Saltings and coastal stability – a biologist's view.* Proceedings of Conference of River Engineers, Cranfield. Unpublished.

Ranwell, D.S. 1964. *Spartina* saltmarshes in southern England. III. Rates of establishment, succession and nutrient supply at Bridgwater Bay, Somerset. *J. Ecol.,* **52,** 95–105.

Ranwell, D.S. 1967. World resources of *Spartina townsendii (sensu lato)* and economic use of *Spartina* marshland. *J. appl. Ecol.,* **4,** 239–256.

Ranwell, D.S. & Downing, B.M. 1960. The use of dalapon and substituted urea herbicides for control of seed bearing *Spartina* (cord grass) in intertidal zones of estuarine marsh. *Weeds,* **8,** 78–88.

Smith, J.S. 1982. The *Spartina* communities of the Cromarty Firth. *Trans. bot. Soc. Edinb.,* **44,** 27–30.

Stapf, O. 1913. Townsend's grass or ricegrass. *Proc. Bournemouth nat. Sci. Soc.,* **5,** 76–82.

Tubbs, C.R. 1980. Processes and impacts in the Solent. In: *The Solent estuarine system.* (Publication Series C no. 22.) Swindon: Natural Environment Research Council.

Tubbs, C. 1984. *Spartina* on the south coast: an introduction. In: Spartina anglica *in Great Britian,* edited by J.P. Doody, 3–4. (Focus on nature conservation no. 5.) Attingham: Nature Conservancy Council.

Printed in the United Kingdom for HMSO
Dd290442 3.90 C20 488 12521